The Rise and Fall of a La Scala Diva

The Rise and Fall of a La Scala Diva

by

Marjorie Wright

JANUS PUBLISHING COMPANY

First published in Great Britain 2006
by Janus Publishing Company Ltd,
105-107 Gloucester Place,
London W1U 6BY

www.januspublishing.co.uk

British Library Cataloguing-in-Publication Data
A catalogue record for this book is available from the British Library

ISBN 10: 1 85756 612 2
ISBN 13: 978 185756 612 3

Cover Design: David Vallance

Printed and bound in Great Britain

In loving memory of Brendan

Contents

Chapter 1

Irish Childhood

The year I was born Hitler and Mosley were indoctrinating Nazism throughout Europe, Bonny and Clyde were shot, Fred Perry won Wimbledon, the composer Edward Elgar died, while in Belfast a budding musician screamed and kicked her way into an unsuspecting world.

Having reached the age of forty-three, my mother assumed she was menopausal, until she went to the doctor, who had a nasty surprise for her.

"Mrs Wright," he said, "you are five months pregnant!"

After they recovered from the shock my parents were over the moon, since they had given up hope of having another child after their second, two-year-old daughter Joan, died of pneumonia.

When I arrived, I was such a bundle of misery that my sister Helen, eight years my senior said: "She's horrible. We can't call her Joy." And so, they changed my name to "Marjorie Winifred", which, in time, became "Marge".

My lungs exuded strange sounds from the day I was born, when I yelled and howled so much that I had to be fed every two hours. It wasn't until a kind friend suggested a dose of slippery elm food that my parents managed to get any sleep at all.

The death of a child is a devastating blow to any family, and my family was no exception. After Joan died Belfast held so many tragic memories for my parents and sister that the family moved to Portadown when I was three.

Now renowned for its annual Drumcree shenanigans, there are few happy memories of our stay there. All I can remember is the menacing drone of German planes, in the early 1940s, as they passed over our house *en route* to Belfast. By the time they had deposited their bombs, Helen and I were already huddled together in her bed waiting for their return journey along the same flight route. I shall never forget that terrible Easter Tuesday night in 1942, when my family and I stood at our landing window watching Belfast burn, after enemy bombers had mistaken a reservoir for Harland and Wolff's shipyard.

Our brand new semi-detached house was one of four, conveniently situated beside Portadown Football Club, of which my father was a devoted supporter. The season had barely finished when the beating of huge Lambeg drums – poised over equally enormous bellies – could be heard all over the area in preparation for "the twelfth" – the annual 12th July Orange procession.

Our lives were uneventful until, one Saturday afternoon, two soldiers out on manoeuvres from a nearby camp called at our house asking for water. They were so charming that my parents invited them to share our rations with us over Sunday lunch, after which they became part of the family. To repay our hospitality, the soldiers created a vegetable plot at the side of our house. Unaware of my father's dislike of gardening, they went away for a few days, leaving him with the simple task of planting potatoes. Little did they know that although he came from an agricultural background he was also allergic to spades and shovels.

My father was one of the most intelligent people I have ever met. When it came to manual labour, he pretended to be so helpless that others either finished the job for him, or never asked him again. Nevertheless, he obeyed orders and planted the "spuds". It wasn't until our garden drew the attention of onlookers that my mother's curiosity got the better of her. To her horror, he had piled soil on top of each potato to create a row of "pyramids". He was vindicated when his potatoes were considered to be the best of that season. When the lawn needed to be mowed, my father would only cut half of it – he was too busy chatting to neighbours and friends – so he was relieved of that chore, too.

My life really took off when we moved southwards to the busy market town of Newry, within sight of the famous Mountains of Mourne. When I am asked where it is, I find it easier to say, "On the border, halfway between Belfast and Dublin", whereas forty miles south of Belfast and sixty north of Dublin would be more accurate.

On approaching the town from the Belfast road, the first building which attracts the eye, is the imposing Town Hall, erected on a bridge over the Clanrye river. Because it is built over water, and not on land, the Newry and Mourne Council is exempt from paying rates. Straddling the two counties of Armagh and Down, it has a special place in my heart, because it was in its homely concert hall that I won the medals and scholarship which paved the way to an international career.

After I inherited my sister's bike, which was far too big for me, I would ride round the town, through which the Clanrye river and Newry canal – the first to be constructed in the British Isles – flow side by side into the Albert Basin. There I used to watch the boats being unloaded before their cargo, usually coal and timber, was transported up the canal by barge.

Following the narrow road and stretch of water along the coast, I would reach the village of Omeath, at the foot of the Cooley Mountains, in the Irish Republic. The view from there, across Carlingford Lough to Warrenpoint, with the Mourne Mountains in the background, is just amazing. Nowadays, the Albert Basin no longer accommodates sea traffic, since Warrenpoint, with its easier access to the open sea, was developed into a thriving, cross-border port.

We lacked for nothing during post-war rationing because of my intrepid mother's smuggling schemes, into which my innocent father was often lured. On the pretence of a "wee drive out", he regularly drove us twelve miles to Dundalk, in the Irish Republic, where, while we went shopping, he would fill up the car with cheap petrol. Poor man, he hardly recognised us when we met up again, looking much fatter than when he had left us, as a result of a "padding" visit to the ladies loo. Once the appetising "forbidden fruits" appeared on the kitchen table, my father was so angry that he threatened to curtail our excursions to the Irish Republic. The ban also included his own family home in County Monaghan, where the customs men on border patrol would joke that my normally slim aunt, looking heavily pregnant on crossing the border, would return shortly afterwards after a quick delivery! When rebuked, my mother would say: "You don't object to eating what we bring home!"

In case you think we were greedy, we did remember our friends "across the water" who were more severely rationed. On one occasion my mother posted a chicken, with strict instructions to look out for the "stuffing", but the pair of silk stockings was not discovered until it was too late to rescue them from the oven.

My mother was, as they say in Ulster, "great craic". She was also responsible for my impromptu singing debut, on a "day out" to a County Down resort, Newcastle, at the foot of the Mournes. My father had taken my sister for a walk, leaving my mother and me to enjoy the Pierrot troupe, who were entertaining a large crowd in a pavilion on the promenade. By the time they returned, the scene had dramatically changed. During their absence my mother had already entered me for a talent competition, which I won with the current hit, *I've Got Sixpence*.

"Do you see who's up there?" exclaimed my horrified father.

"Yes", I put her there," was his wife's reply.

And so, with the mighty Slieve Donard – the highest peak of the Mournes – looking down on me, I sang my first notes in front of a rapturous audience, at the age of seven.

Music was the food of love in our house, closely followed by soccer, current affairs, and the latest "goings on" on both sides of the border.

My paternal family were planters who came over from Yorkshire in 1610. They settled in Gola in County Monaghan, from where, over the centuries, they gradually expanded into the counties of Fermanagh and Tyrone. The Wrights were primarily landowners, clergymen and writers – the Rev. James Wright wrote a controversial book on *The Brontes in Ireland* towards the end of the nineteenth century. But it wasn't until my grandfather married the ebullient and talented Margaret Davidson that music became part of everyday life at Elvey, the lovely white-washed house which my grandfather bought in 1885. Now owned by my farming cousin – where the family tradition of making music together is still carried on – it is situated on the side of the road between Monaghan and the County Tyrone border.

Unfortunately, I knew neither of my grandparents, because they died long before I was born – Granny was in her late forties when she had my father, the youngest of ten children – but the stories about her are legendary. Being a talented dancer, my grandmother led the dances at the great houses throughout the county, while at Elvey she held barn dances every Saturday night for neighbours and friends. She would often be seen riding side-saddle over the fields on her horse, distributing food to those in need.

Among my ubiquitous grandmother's talents was the gift of perfect pitch, the ability to pitch notes without the aid of an instrument. She enthralled her children and grandchildren with her infectious sense of rhythm, and, in the absence of percussion instruments, substituted them with fireside utensils.

Unfortunately, some of my cousins took after the Wrights and were, therefore, not endowed with Davidson musicianship. On one particular night my grandmother, having retired early for the night, could be heard banging the floor with her stick to put a stop to the noise downstairs,where my cousins were having a sing-song.

"Will you tell the Lissadavil (the name of their house) ones to stop singing?" she shouted down. "They are a quarter tone out!"

There was also a blood link between my parents' families. My maternal grandmother was the niece of my father's mother, which meant that the Davidson perfect pitch was also passed down to my mother's family, the McGuffins. Because of this inheritance, I can sight-read music at speed. It can, however, be a handicap when music has to be transposed, since I often have difficulty if I have to depart from the original key.

It was, therefore, no surprise when my mother decided to develop my voice herself. It was a challenge which she relished since, in those days, married women were unable to teach in schools, depriving her of the chance to exercise her considerable teaching skills.

Under her guidance, many medals were won at the local festival, or *Feis* as it is known in most parts of Ireland. It was a different story when I went to face stiffer competition in Belfast. The size of the Assembly Hall was a far cry from the homeliness of Newry

Town Hall, apart from the fact that I detested the set piece. Being a Cancerian, I can't stand rejection, so when I was placed bottom of the class, I vowed never to return there, which, in later years, I did. With hindsight, it is ironic to think that when I eventually became a professional singer, I had to sing impalpable music, just to keep the wolf from the door.

One of my fondest memories of those happy days at Newry *Feis* was the day I won the under-twelve solo with a delightful song called *The Paper Boat*. But nothing eclipsed the sensation I caused in the verse-speaking section, when I injected a bit of zip into W.B. Yeats' beautiful poem *The Lake Isle of Innisfree*. Having endured thirty-two competitors identically reciting it in the same monotonous drone, I decided to raise the tone of the verse to unheard of heights. My shocked mother said that I thoroughly deserved to be publicly humiliated by the adjudicator on my use of soliloquy. For days, all my mother would say was: "I'll never get over the disgrace", but she did. In time, she became immune to all the crazy things that happened to me.

"If there's an awkward way round life, Marjorie will find it," she would say.

Friday nights were a great occasion in our house, when my father's three mates would arrive to rehearse for their forthcoming male-quartet performances. My mother was both vocal chief and chef, while my father was second tenor. I would be sent to bed early so as not to cause havoc, yet rewarded by the lovely strains of *Eileen Aroon* lulling me to sleep. In later years I discovered that they were affectionately known as the "Grapefruit Quartet" because of the amount of tinned grapefruit they consumed to soothe their aching throats.

People simply will not believe me when I tell them that I was once a shy and confused child with a terrible stammer, of which my family was unaware. I never faltered within the security of my happy home environment, but outside was a different matter. Indeed, I thought that my secret was safe, until our butcher, a family friend, decided to voice his concern about my affliction – for that it was – to my father. I don't know how he could have noticed it; when my mother sent me out "to do the messages" as they say in Ulster, I assiduously wrote down everything on a piece of paper before handing it over the counter.

As a result of this revelation, my parents, who had decided to keep the butcher's information to themselves, sent me to the wonderful Miss Kielty, whose elocution classes transformed my life. Not only did my self-confidence reach new heights, but I made new friends, with whom I could share my new passion for the stage. I was so terrified of the unknown, that a former neighbour remembers me deliberately crossing the road to avoid speaking to him.

"You've come a long way, Marjorie," he said. "I simply can't believe it is you when I hear you chatting away on the radio."

Newry was, and still is, a great cultural centre in which young talent is expertly developed. My parents were ardent drama and music buffs, and rarely missed an opportunity to take my sister and me to cultural events in the Town Hall. There were memorable productions of plays, such as *Hamlet, Pygmalion, Blythe Spirit* – to name but a few – by the award-winning Newpoint Players, and Gilbert and Sullivan operas by the Newry Musical Society, while Newry Philharmonic, in which both my parents participated, catered for lovers of oratorios, like Handel's *Messiah*, Bach's *Christmas Oratorio* and Haydn's *Creation*.

Years later, as a professional soloist, I returned to perform with the Philharmonic, with my parents still singing in the chorus, just as they had done in my youth.

My love for the piano, which I had been playing since the age of three, was cemented after my mother took me to see the film *The Seventh Veil*, starring Ann Todd and the husky-voiced James Mason, with whom I fell madly in love. It was the tale of a concert pianist who, pressured by her stricter guardian, played by my hero, studied at the Royal College of Music, London, before achieving success and succumbing to her guardian's hidden and softer side. I spent many happy hours imagining myself in the same role, dressed in a long, flowing gown, playing Grieg's *Piano Concerto* to adoring fans at the Royal Albert Hall, while my knight in shining armour waited to greet me in my dressing room with a bouquet of red roses. As the years rolled by, and dreams became reality, not once did I have such an off-stage encounter. Instead, I discovered that one is so drained after a performance, all one wants to do is to go home, have a drink and unwind.

In the early years, school wasn't much fun. I was never out of trouble for talking too much, not studying and preventing those who wished to from doing so. On the other hand, they benefited from my lunchtime concerts in a room beside the headmaster's office, where I gathered those interested round a piano and taught them how to chant boring French and Latin verbs to my boogie-woogie piano arrangements; little did we know that our patient headmaster was our greatest fan!

But all good things must come to an end; and mine did, after my long-suffering father delivered an ultimatum. He had had enough: Either I apply myself to the printed matter, or remain at school until the necessary exam results were achieved – even if it meant remaining there into old age.

My father rarely raised his voice, being outnumbered by three women, but when he did we stood to attention. He was nobody's fool and, unknown to us all, had been observing my tactics for some time.

"It takes brains to think up mischievous pranks like yours," he said. His words filled me with guilt as he spoke, since I worshiped the ground he walked on. "Why don't you put that energy into studying, instead of causing trouble? You might even enjoy it."

There and then, I re-opened abandoned books and discovered that my father was right. Not only did I actually enjoy studying, but school as well. Even the teachers were amazed at the change in their wayward student.

Newry Grammar was a very happy school – one could affectionately describe it as a co-educational St. Trinian's. The girls had a tough time coping with the boys' banter and pranks, but we survived. It was the ideal environment for a reticent and confused girl like me. Because I had no brothers, I appreciated the company of boys, who, affectionately, would tease me, just to see my reaction. Yet, not one of my fellow pupils would have even thought of bullying me; in fact, they never batted an eyelid when I cccc...ed and mmmmm...ed, until I nearly died of shame and embarrassment.

The person who did bully me was our domestic science teacher who hated the air I breathed. To spare her family embarrassment I shall refer to her by her Christian name, Leo. Such were her vitriolic attacks on me that, decades later, I discovered that other pupils used to keep their families up to date on the latest Wright-versus-Leo war of attrition.

Around this difficult period in my life, I decided to follow in my father's footsteps and learn the violin. He rarely used his, except to accompany my sister while she attempted to study her piano pieces. Poor girl, she didn't stand a chance, what with our father playing over her shoulder, and our spaniel dog barking at both of them.

Every Saturday, I would strap the coveted instrument on to the back of my bicycle and head to County Armagh, and my teacher's lovely home, Walden Lodge, surrounded by luscious, green fields on the outskirts of Newry. Apart from being a fabulous teacher, Mrs Henry exuded culture and charm, and I just loved her. Some of her own family also played in the Walden Orchestra, named after their home. It wasn't long before I joined them as a second violin player, participating in many choral society performances, for which we provided the orchestral accompaniment. It was in this stimulating and caring atmosphere that my passion for oratorio and orchestral music was nurtured. I loved it so much that I decided to become a professional. However, I was denied this chance, partly because my voice took priority over both violin and piano, and also because I never again found a violin teacher, or, indeed, any other tutor of the calibre of the ones eventually I left behind in Ireland.

It was during one of these rural Saturday afternoon rehearsals that, in complete innocence, I happened to tell a lady, with whom I shared a music stand, about the chaos I had caused at school during a disastrous culinary attempt in Leo's kitchen. In my endeavour to unload my burden onto a willing ear, I completely forgot that Molly, my enthralled listener was my teacher's next door neighbour! But that was only the prelude to an encounter which was to change my whole life. The following week Molly gleefully entertained the teacher's elegant coffee morning guests with the story of my culinary escapade. Unfortunately for me, it brought the house down.

To this very day, those present at the lesson which followed that coffee morning remember all hell breaking loose in the kitchen.

9

Fortunately, our headmaster, affectionately known as the "Boss", could hear it in the next room as he tried to teach physics above the almighty roaring and shouting coming out of the kitchen, where the maniacal "victim" was in full flight.

"Who do you think you are?" she bellowed. "You mimicked and made fun of me. You even lied that you made oatmeal biscuits, when it was soda bread (an Irish recipe made with soda and buttermilk) that you massacred".

As I stood there at the top of the class, more verbal abuse was hurled at me, until, having ended her vitriol, I climbed out of the kitchen window – Leo's way of disposing of unwanted pupils – and out onto the hockey pitch. The only other exit would have been through the physics lab next door, thereby revealing all to the Boss, who had heard most of it anyway. The unforgettable hate exuding from Leo that day left an indelible mark, and imbued me with a distrust of females which has lasted to this very day.

Naturally, there had to be an inquest into my kitchen drama. In those days, the teacher's word was law, and children didn't bring home tales from school, since they, and not the teacher, were the presumed culprits. But the Boss was different. He believed in hearing both sides of the story before passing judgement. It was therefore natural that my parents, on receiving a summons to the headmaster's office said: "What has she done *now?*"

At the beginning of the meeting my mother explained that my propensity towards story-telling and impersonation, which, by the way, I inherited from her, had to be taken into account before blaming the teacher for whom, as a qualified one herself, she had considerable sympathy. But the Boss was *adamant.* Not only was he aware of the domestic science teacher's tactics on those she disliked, but her persistent bullying of me was well known throughout the school, and, as a result, I was immediately removed from her class. I'm sure she didn't miss me; people like her lose no time in finding other vulnerable victims.

In later years I not only became a respected cook, although culinary stories from my hilarious dinner parties are still doing the rounds by those who survived, and, with the help of easy Vogue patterns, made some rather stunning outfits.

Naturally, a void had been left in my timetable, but there was no need to worry, since the Boss had a master plan in mind. This extraordinary man, who cared so much for his students, had noticed my participation in the various musical events around Newry. He himself was not musical, and went to such concerts only in his role as a headmaster. But my enthusiasm for what I loved hadn't escaped his notice, coupled with the knowledge that I had just won a piano bursary at Newry *Feis*. And so, while my mates sweated in the kitchen, I travelled every Monday afternoon to the beautiful cathedral city of Armagh. There, after my piano lesson, I would have a look round the cathedrals and shops until it was time to catch the bus home.

In those days, it was a rare treat for a girl of fifteen to be so independently privileged. And so, imbued with enthusiasm, I took full advantage of it and won yet another, more financially rewarding bursary to study with the celebrated Belfast teacher and composer Dorothy Parke.

Considering that the school didn't have a music department at that time, the Boss acted ingeniously. Our only access to the world of music was a mixed singing class, where discipline was non-existent. Eventually, when I had to cope with unruly pupils in my own singing classes, I wondered if divine retribution was punishing me for all the naughty pranks we played on our singing teacher. Class singing is one of the most difficult subjects to cope with; once mouths are open, it is easy to transmute sounds into rowdy behaviour. Medals have been awarded for less valour.

Alas, Newry Grammar no longer exists. Some years after I left, it moved to another building, when, on changing to Newry High School, it later became one of the first integrated state schools in the town. Not a day passes that I am not grateful for the excellent academic and cultural education I got in Newry. If it hadn't been for that wonderful start in life, and the incident in "Hell's' Kitchen" I would never have achieved what I have. During the writing of this book, Newry was deservedly awarded city status.

Music was obviously destined to form a major part of my life. After I left school, I headed for Belfast to enroll at a teacher at a teacher training college, where I distinguished myself as a complete misfit. In order to remain there, one had to pass a simple maths test; but because I was incapable of anything above the most rudimentary arithmetic, the entire venture was a waste of time.

I hated primary teaching and spent study time driving the other hostel inmates to distraction with my violin practice. Our student accommodation was quite Dickensian, ruled over with a rod of iron by a matron, who instilled discipline by prowling the corridors rattling her massive bunch of keys. Considering that we were no longer children, it was worse than boarding school. We even had to be in by 11 pm, otherwise, we were severely reprimanded.

Our particular building, known as "The Bungalows", was the most rigidly run on the campus. The students' rooms, at ground level, had bars on the windows, making us feel that we were under the surveillance of a prison warden. The beds in the "cells" were unforgettable. They were surrounded by bars, resembling cradles, except for the side one used to get into the wretched contraption. I dreaded Monday mornings when we had to collect our clean sheets, along with our allocation of butter, eggs and sugar, because rationing was still in force. Then the most complicated way of bed-making began.

Instead of beginning the normal routine of sheets first and blankets on top, the situation was reversed. Then, they were neatly tucked under the mattress, before being turned upside down, with sheets at the bottom and blankets on top, to look like a "normal" bed.

The piece of earthenware which amused us most in this den of antiquity was the chamber pot, which one kept under one's bed. The only time mine left my room was when another student was ill in bed and each one of us brought her a present of a "wee pot". On recovery, she didn't speak to us for a week. But, in spite of everything, we had a lot of fun in my unofficial "year out", and life-long friendships were formed.

It was during that memorable year that yet another decision was made which was to change the entire course of my life. Dorothy Parke used to ask me to sing the very beautiful songs she had composed before sending them for publication. One of them, *Kilkeel*, I simply adored because it was about the Mourne

Mountains, of which Dorothy and I were so fond. At that point, I was not so keen on singing, focusing more on the piano and Beethoven sonatas. One Saturday afternoon, however, while I was immersed in one of them, Dorothy stopped me in full flight."You'll never make a pianist," she said. "But, as you haven't a bad wee voice, you might have a better chance as a singer."

I felt as my left arm had just been cut off, since I lived for my lessons with Dorothy, and was devastated at the thought of exchanging piano for singing lessons. However, wonderful as she was, one didn't argue with Dorothy. Before I could think straight, she had lifted the phone to her friend John Patterson, one of Belfast's best singing teachers, and persuaded him to include me in his exclusive list of students. He was another who, in typical Ulster fashion, wasted no time. In the first months of teaching, he and his wife Mina entered me for the mezzo-soprano solo at the Belfast Festival. I won the competition, along with a distinction in an Associated Board singing exam. This, in turn, enabled me to enter for a scholarship to one of the schools of music in London.

The burning question was: what we were going to about my commitment to the training college and government grant? After long deliberation with my mother and my teachers – my father wanted no part in it – it was decided to gamble, and risk burning all our bridges.

After I was expelled from college because I failed my exams, I found a temporary teaching job in a country primary school, perched on a hill outside Newry. With hindsight, 1953 was one of the happiest and most productive years in my life. I adored teaching children ranging from four to seven years old, and practiced the songs, which my teachers and I had chosen for the Associated Board scholarship, until my neighbours began humming the tunes themselves. But the icing on the cake was being left alone (my friends were either working or at university in Belfast) to enjoy Warrenpoint, where we had been living for four years.

Throughout my extensive travels to scenic countries, I couldn't resist comparing them with the beauty of the County Down coastline – the "South Down Riviera", as we call it. This stretches from Newry to Warrenpoint, and then, along panoramic scenery, through Rostrevor and Kilkeel to Newcastle, home of the famous

Royal County Down golf links. Tiger Woods often practices there in the run-up to the British Open championship.

When I taught singing in Como, my Italian students used to laugh when I would tell them that their lovely lake, also surrounded by mountains, reminded me of Carlingford Lough. It is impossible to tire of the view from the Warrenpoint sea front, with the Mournes to the left, and the Cooley Mountains, in the Republic of Ireland, to the right. In winter, when the mountains are covered in snow, it looks like Switzerland; in summer, one can imagine one is in the Bahamas; in autumn, there is the unbelievable pleasure of watching the harvest moon rise from behind the Mournes, to cast it's reflection over the still Lough.

Narrowater, which is self-explanatory, is an artist's paradise, with its medieval castle, full of folklore. I know I have arrived home when, almost at the end of the carriage-way from Newry I come across its amazing beauty, with the mountains in the background. In Autumn, the colours on the mountain, leading from Narrowater to Newry, have to be seen to be believed; they can range from brown and red, to orange and bronze, while a rowing boat can carry one across from this narrow stretch of water to the Irish Republic in a matter of minutes. Narrowater, along with the motor-boat from Warrenpoint to Omeath, carried many a clandestine luxury when smuggling was at its peak.

From then on, filled with fresh air, hill climbing and my mum's home cooking, the preparation began for the greatest gamble of my life, culminating in one spring evening, when, along with another student of Dorothy Parke's, I set off across the water for London, where my sister Helen – by then working there – met us at the start of an action-packed week at the Royal College of Music, just down the steps from the Royal Albert Hall. Days of intense competition followed, during which we had to return at the end of each evening session to find out who would go through to the next round. Miraculously, I reached the finals, after which I was packed off back to Ireland to await the outcome.

At last, after a week of unbearable suspense, I saw Joe the postman (who had been warned what to expect) speeding towards me, as I was on my way to work, with an envelope in his hand. With bated breath, he watched as I opened it and read:

"You have been awarded an Associated Board scholarship to the Royal College of Music", the very one of my choice.

The post delivery was late that morning in Warrenpoint. But nobody cared. By the time the postman had celebrated with my parents over a cup of tea, news had already spread round the town. Joe was bombarded with questions about my reaction to the news. "What did she say?" "How did she look?"

"I don't know," was his reply. "We were too busy dancing an Irish jig in the middle of the road."

The rousing surprise send-off at Warrenpoint station was worthy of a film script. Friends and well-wishers, who included the clergy no less, showered me in confetti from head to toe. It certainly eased the heartbreak I was suffering at leaving home and the lovely scenery, for which I was to yearn thereafter.

And so, amid much hilarity and tears all round, I set off on my journey, surrounded by luggage and confetti – like a bride without a husband – ready to take on the world single-handedly. In the years that followed, I often wondered if my piano teacher's decision to make someone like me into a prima donna had been a wise one. But at that time I was young, full of adventure, and ready to tackle anything. As the train slowly pulled out of the station, and my friends, still waving and shouting, could no longer be seen, I suddenly realised that a happy chapter in my life had just closed.

On that balmy September night, I felt lonely and sad as I stood out on the deck of the Belfast to Liverpool boat, the *Ulster Prince*, as it slowly made its way down Belfast Lough to the open sea, with the shimmering lights of Islandmagee and Donaghadee gradually disappearing from sight. I tried to imagine what it must have been like in 1912, when cheers rang out along the shores of that same lough, as the *Titanic* sailed from Harland and Wolff's shipyard to begin her maiden voyage from Southampton.

Next morning, after a smooth crossing and a good night's sleep, I awoke, refreshed and exhilarated, to the beginning of a challenging new era.

Chapter 2

London

Everything fell into my lap as I floated round my new-found metropolis on "cloud nine". Having gone there to compete for the scholarship, it wasn't an entirely new experience. Businessmen hadn't discarded their bowler hats and umbrellas, while the ladies were as elegantly coiffured and dressed as ever.

Not long after my arrival – I have always been mad about fashion – I decided to take the plunge and discard my country bumpkin image. My self-confidence soared when, on my return to college, my fellow students gasped at the transformation from full skirts and flat-heeled shoes to a straight skirt and neat court shoes. To complete the make-over, I had my hair styled in the latest "Italian look", short, wavy, and without a parting. Later, when I had more money, I invested in an "A line" dress, with the tight-fitting bodice extending to the hips, from which a full, "Pyramid" type skirt would billow out. Fashion in the middle 1950s and early 1960s was about taste and class. Chanel suits, with their short jackets and knee-length skirts were gracing the cat-walks, along with demure, figure-hugging evening gowns, setting the trend for the outfits worn by Jackie Kennedy when her husband became American president.

I shared a room with my sister in the up-market hostel in posh Knightsbridge, where she met her future husband, just round the corner from Harvey Nichols and the Hyde Park Hotel. Unfortunately, we had to move from there when the building was taken over by a consortium and made into luxury flats. Ironically, in my student days, I lived in areas that I could never have afforded once I became a struggling musician. On leaving Knightsbridge, I moved to an even grander abode in Hyde Park Gate, overlooking Kensington Gardens, within walking distance from College, and practically next door to Sir Winston Churchill. Living in such an elegant quarter, and among such distinguished neighbours – Kensington Palace, where members of the royal family live, was only down the road – gave me such a posh accent that I nearly, but not quite, lost my Ulster one.

It was the era of the "stiff upper lip", epitomising everything that was English, until the first ship from the West Indies arrived in Plymouth in 1955. Over the years, many more legal, and illegal, immigrants, looking for new opportunities and a better lifestyle, were to converge on England to transform it into today's more multi-cultural society.

My first day at the Royal College of Music was not what I had expected. To begin with, my introduction to my singing professor was catastrophic. A Trevor Howard look-a-like with an Oxford accent, he taught with a Galois cigarette hanging out of the side of his mouth, while his students sang through the smoke. His dislike of Irish people was obvious. He treated me, and another girl from Belfast, as if we had just come out of the nearest bog.

"Who told you were a mezzo-soprano?" he said. "You'll never make a singer, because your mouth is too small. If I'd been on that adjudicating panel," he drawled on, "you'd never have got that scholarship."

You can imagine how relieved I was that he wasn't!

My next appointment was with my violin professor, a tall and charming gentleman, with a Humpty-Dumpty tummy. He wasn't amused when a shower of confetti, clandestinely placed there at my Irish send-off, cascaded out of my violin case, straight onto the floor. By the time I had gone down to the kitchen to get a dustpan and brush, and cleaned up the mess – on my knees – there was little left of the three-quarters of an hour, lesson. That was all we got.

Throughout my three years studying with my singing professor, I never questioned his decision to undo my Belfast teacher's sound Italian-styled technique and replace it with his own brand. What reason had I to doubt him? He was senior singing professor at one Britain's most prestigious musical institutions, from which many world-famous musicians had emerged. In the space of a week, a fixed smile transformed me from a mellifluous, deep-throated mezzo-contralto into a high-pitched soprano. Such sounds were produced by pushing out my rib cage, while holding on like grim death to my diaphragm. Some of the sounds emerging from that room were described by an outsider as "coming out of a veterinary surgery". When I myself started to teach, I was sure that mine was more like an abattoir! By then I had discovered that ugly sounds pave the way for beautiful ones.

During the Christmas break, parents and former singing teachers were horrified at the vocal transformation and facial contortions I presented to them. But I wouldn't listen to them. If I had, I wouldn't have amassed the tips for my book, *How To Be A Bad Singer*, on how to avoid straining the voice.

Two decades passed before I was allowed to sing in the richer and more comfortable lower part of my voice; yet, despite all our misunderstandings about vocal production, and his anti-Irish approach, my teacher and I shared some memorable moments. Bursting with pride, he made a rare appearance in the college's lovely white-panelled concert hall to hear me sing Richard Strauss's *Four Last Songs* with the First Orchestra in 1958, before winning, in the same year, the coveted Clara Butt leaving award for singers. Some of my friends made a secret recording of the Strauss songs. To do so they had to stop the hall's great clock because its ticking could be heard above the glorious music during rehearsal. Richard Seale, one of the "engineers", was later to become the distinguished organist of Salisbury Cathedral

I never quite understood why composition was included in my RCM curriculum, especially since I ended up in the "premier league" with the distinguished English composer Dr Herbert Howells as my professor. Dr Howells was an elegantly dressed man of small stature, with wavy white hair, who simply oozed charm. He loved Irish "craic", and made sure that each term my lesson preceded that of Derek Bell, my old pal from our musical days back home. One morning Derek and I accidentally spilt coffee over Dr Howells' smart blue suit which he had specially worn that day to meet the distinguished German composer, Paul Hindemith.

Somehow, Derek and I, with help from the college kitchen's Mrs Mop department, managed to restore his Saville suit to it's pristine condition.

Music lovers all over the world were heartbroken when Derek suddenly died in October, 2002, just after he had finished touring with the famous Irish group, the Chieftains.

He and I first met when, as teenagers, I was a violinist and he the oboe player in the Walden Orchestra – mentioned in the previous chapter. He was indeed a 'friend in need' when my own career went temporarily pear-shaped. To help me get back on top, he offered to compose a special piece of music displaying the qualities in my voice and crazy personality which he admired. We had planned a series of concerts to include some of Dr Howells' wonderful music for voice and piano, along with the new composition for me, but unfortunately, he died before it was completed. Apart from our life-long friendship, I miss his wonderful letters, written in his distinctive scrawl, and addressed to Dame Marjorie Wright, OBE, to boost my morale when the chips were down.

Although I was never among Dr Howells' star students, I learnt a lot about composing music, when we weren't discussing Irish and English rugby and cricket. One day, during my lesson, I happened to mention that my mother was waiting for me in the students' canteen. I thought nothing more about it until, having rejoined her, the canteen door burst open to reveal Dr Howells.

"Mrs Wright," he said, approaching her with outstretched hand, "I just had to see who produced Marjorie."

As well as his position at RCM, Dr Howells was also music director at St. Paul's Girls' School, Hammersmith. When he invited me to sing there, he showed me the room where the composer Gustav Holst, his predecessor, wrote *The Planets*. He had a special reason for taking me there: Holst's astrological predictions were so authentic that one evening, while having a drink together, he saw in Howells' hand the death of his ten-year-old son. He only told his friend after the tragedy, from which Dr Howells never recovered, although he had a daughter, of whom he was so proud, the actress Ursula Howells.

In my third year at RCM, I did the teacher graduate course. My singing professor nearly hit the roof when I told him, since he had expected me to go into the opera school.

"If you are going to take out an insurance policy you'll never make it," he said. "You should be in the opera school, and not with your head in books!"

But he lost the fight, not only because my father declared that "he wasn't going to have an uneducated musician in the family", but the education committee in Belfast, which was subsidising my grant, wanted value for its money. I had already wasted one, and they weren't going to risk another. After I became a graduate of the Royal Schools of Music, I picked up my suitcase and headed for Heathrow. I shall never forget my parent's faces at Aldergrove, now Belfast International Airport.

"I got it, I got it," I shouted and waved, as my parents anxiously watched me coming down the steps of the plane. It was worth it, just for that moment.

Before I left college, the organiser of the graduate course told me that she had just seen an advertisement for a part-time singing teacher at Roedean, the famous girls' school, high above the cliffs, just outside Brighton. When I went there for my interview, I couldn't believe my eyes when I saw the size of the lovely, stone-bricked building, stretching across the Downs. To me, it looked more like a large country mansion than a school; so you can imagine my delight when I was offered a job in this idyllic setting. Teaching at Roedean was a great privilege. Only the mighty winds off the sea disturbed the serenity of the school, which, at times, could be compared to a draughty railway station. A student's mother even had to hold her hat on walking along an indoor corridor. The girls addressed the teachers as "madam", which greatly embarrassed me, since some of the sixth-formers, were not much younger than me.

Because I was only part time, I travelled down once a week on the Brighton Belle – a train with plush Pullman carriages, which has since been withdrawn from service. I only stayed one night at the school, making it feel more like a holiday outing than going to work. In no way did Roedean resemble the St. Trinian's films; on the contrary, discipline was so strict that one could have heard a pin drop. All one had to do was teach. Nevertheless, there was a great atmosphere in the school, in which even the housemistresses' Pekinese dogs were included; if you didn't get on with them, you didn't get on with the owners!

As it happened, the presentation of my Clara Butt leaving award took place during my first term at Roedean. When the ballet-mistress, affectionately known as the "Barronova", heard that I had to curtsey before Queen Elizabeth, the Queen Mother, she immediately took me under her wing. Her task was not an easy one since, according to an in-law, "the Wrights aren't too good on their pins"!

Nevertheless, against the odds, we persevered to the point of my curtseying to everyone in sight, even with heavy books in my arms until, at last the great day approached, when it was time for a "girls' chat" to decide, not what dress I would wear, but what type of underwear! Somewhat taken back, I listened intently while the Barronova, told me the sad tale of a former Roedean girl who, as she was about to rise up after curtseying before the Queen and Prince Philip, discovered that the back suspender of her right nylon stocking – there were no tights in those days – had become entangled with the front one of her left one. The poor girl remained trapped, until a palace attendant arrived to lift her up out of her agony. Fortunately, it didn't happen to me because tights were then in fashion. I wore them under the lovely blue dress – with a satin sheen and belle-shaped skirt – with a bow at the front, which I bought in Harrods. I should have taken the Queen Mother's minute size into consideration; I towered over her in a pair of shoes with very high heels. The photograph taken that day shows her, in her customary platform-soles, reaching up to me with the prize in her hand. Thank goodness I didn't repeat my dress rehearsal performance when I was so busy thinking about my wonky feet, and the Barronova's warning, that I left Sir Ernest Bullock – the then director of RCM, who was deputising for the Queen Mum – still holding the prize!

My mother flew over from Ireland for the combined celebration of the prize-giving and the birth of her first grandchild – my lovely nephew Richard – the previous week. Like me, she talked to everybody and anybody. While I was having tea with the Queen Mother, if you'll excuse the name-dropping, my mother, left to her own devices, chatted up the college professors, who just loved her. Afterwards, she revealed that the highlight of her afternoon was Vaughan Williams's *The Lark Ascending*. When I hear that haunting violin solo, depicting the English countryside, I always think of the pleasure it gave her that day.

Unfortunately, wonderful as Roedean was, I couldn't live on what I was paid. To supplement my earnings, I went from the sublime to the ridiculous when I began teaching violin to an unruly mob at an inner-city London County Council school. Assisted by my head of department, they showed me no mercy. In stark contrast to her charming equivalent at Roedean, this particular music head told me that, apart from being too "posh" for the job, I was full of myself because I had taught at a public school. My flatmates killed themselves laughing when I told them this, because I used to purposely "dress down" in old sweaters and skirts for the LCC school, keeping my "finery" for Roedean.

Everything came to a head when, exasperated by the noise of crashing bridges being attached to brand new violins, I went out and bought a pot of glue, with which I firmly stuck the bridges on to the instruments. Unaware that one should never, ever, touch a violin with glue, I was subsequently sacked, after one of the brats grassed on me. Considering that I became a qualified violin teacher by a stroke of destiny, it's a wonder that I got the job at all.

When I applied to do the GRSM course, I had to choose violin, my second study, because singing lessons were not on the syllabus for the junior exhibitioners course held at RCM on Saturday mornings; in fact, when they were introduced I was the first teacher of the subject. And so, because these young people were taught by the undergraduates as part of their course, the poor kids had me as a violin tutor, which I thoroughly enjoyed, even if they didn't.

As part of the diploma exam, we had to pass an oral, practical exam in our chosen subject. This did not unduly worry my fellow students, because they were all taking their first subject, but my violin playing and knowledge of the instrument left much to be desired. To ease my troubled mind, my friends encouraged me to read a book on violin technique by Herbert Kinsey, a professor at the college, who not only was the examiner but asked questions based on this text.

By the time the oral arrived I could nearly have recited the book, which enhanced my confidence, until I reached the examination room. There I was informed that not only was Mr Kinsey indisposed, but his place would be taken by Harvey Phillips, the senior cello professor at RCM.

I nearly had to resuscitated on the spot! Harvey Phillips may have been one the most popular professors at college, but he knew how badly I played the violin, after I came in too early in an out-of-tune chord, during a performance of a Beethoven symphony with the college orchestra, which he conducted. Under such stressful circumstances I had no other option but to appeal to the Almighty.

Suddenly, my prayers were answered when a frustrated viola player, who knew Harvey Phillips well, came out of the room.

"It's alright for you, Marge," she said. "He knows how bad you are, and what to expect. But for me, it's the end of my diploma."

There and then she poured out her heart to me, telling me about the difficult questions he had thrown at her, as well as the *answers* which he had provided. You can imagine his surprise when I faced the same interrogation with considerable confidence. Years later, however, I confessed to the retired organiser of the course what had happened.

"You would have had passed without the oral," she reassured me; "in fact, you got an A plus in your teaching course."

My flatmates were delighted when I was "relieved" of my instrumental work. Living with my teaching dramas, and me, cannot have been easy. Our flat in Notting Hill Gate was filled to capacity with my Irish friends, who often arrived, unannounced, suitcase in hand, to "look up Marge". My other three mates were "the harem" referred to in James Galway's book. I am sure that the reader is aware that he is the famous Belfast-born flautist. He, my flatmates and I had all been at college together. Before I joined the girls, they had lived in another flat in Gloucester Road, where we would all congregate, chiefly because they were excellent cooks and held great parties. During an Asian flu epidemic, one of the girls found Jimmy, dressed in rose-pink pyjamas, waiting to be nursed. Flatsharing was great fun, and certainly improved one's culinary skills. I could hardly boil an egg when I joined the girls in Notting Hill

Gate, but I soon learnt. In fact, my Irish stews could have taken their place in any school kitchen, along with my meals 'tied up with string', as one friend referred to my beef olives.

The early 1960s were full of innocent fun. Television wasn't the dominant force it is today; drugs were only taken for medicinal purposes; men and women met in coffee bars, and people entertained, without ostentation, at home. Films like *The African Queen*, *The Big Sleep* and *Casablanca*, or shows like *My Fair Lady*, with Julie Andrews and Rex Harrison were the main sources of attraction.

The gap in my income was soon filled when my compatriot, the contralto Jean Allister, introduced me to John McCarthy, the dynamic director of the Ambrosian Singers, who was looking for a second soprano to sing *Cinque Rechants*, by the French composer Oliver Messiaen, at the Promenade concerts. Because it was based on the twelve-tone music system, John was looking for a soprano with perfect pitch and the ability to sight-read at speed. Throughout my career, these "trademarks" were to be the reason why I worked at all. It was some considerable time before I would gain recognition as a singer with a beautiful voice, instead of "just a good musician", who could prop up a recording session, or salvage a crisis.

That introduction to Messiaen may have taken years off my life, but it guaranteed me work and lots of fun with this world-famous group who sang for, and with, the greatest musicians in the world. Many household names unequivocally acknowledge the exceptional musical training and opportunities provided by John McCarthy. I followed in the shadow of Heather Harper and Janet Baker, but I was there with Robert Tear and John Shirley-Quirk, as well as my old friend Gerald English.

During my time with the Ambrosians, I also took part in innumerable concerts and recording sessions, which benefited me throughout my long career. I shall always remember taking part in a recording of Handel's *Messiah*, when Sir Thomas Beecham auditioned and humiliated a young, unknown Joan Sutherland: she still made it to the top, in spite of his antagonism.

My most treasured memory from those wonderful days was in 1962, when sixteen of us took part in the first performance of Benjamin Britten's *War Requiem* in the newly opened Coventry

Cathedral. When Britten realised that the powerful and intricate choral section was beyond the capacity of an amateur choir, he asked John McCarthy to urgently send reinforcements to Coventry. I was one of the lucky people, eight men and eight girls, who, each evening, drove up and down the M1 to Coventry to rehearse for the opening concert. Once we began to sing, the Sheffield Choral Society, gaining confidence as the rehearsals progressed, amalgamated with us to form a very happy unit. It was a different story when we augmented the posh Bach Choir on an Italian tour of the work: they didn't speak to us throughout the entire trip.

Politics also played a dominant part in the first performance of the *Requiem*. Benjamin Britten had written the part for solo soprano for the Russian Galina Vishnevskaya, the wife of the celebrated cellist Mstislav Rostropovich. Because Dietrich Fisher-Dieskau, the great German baritone, was also among the soloists, along with the tenor Peter Pears, the communist regime would not grant permission for Galina Vishnevskaya to sing with a German from West Berlin. Three weeks before the opening performance, my compatriot and pal Heather Harper did what was considered to be virtually impossible, and not only learnt the difficult score, but sang it magnificently. It was a rather emotional experience for the performers looking out through the enormous windows to the silhouette of the old, bomb-scarred cathedral, depicting the theme of reconciliation which Britten expressed in his marvellous *Requiem*. That evening, as the last strains of the work died away in that sombre atmosphere, people just sat and wept.

Eventually, Vishnevskaya was allowed to take part in a recording of the *War Requiem* with Fisher Dieskau in 1963, in which all of the Ambrosians took part, under the name of the London Symphony Chorus and orchestra.

In the early 1960s, during the time when Walter Legge was director of EMI and the Philarmonia orchestra, the Ambrosians participated in numerous recordings with Otto Klemperer, the austere and rather foreboding German maverick. The most memorable of these, mainly because he conducted them at a snail's pace, were the *St. John*, and *St. Matthew Passions*.

26

One morning, in sub-zero temperatures, we all assembled in Walthamstow Town Hall to rehearse for a Festival Hall performance of the *St. Matthew*. We had just begun the first chorus, when John McCarthy came up to me and said: "Marge, do know the solos?"

"Of course, I do," I answered, in a laid-back, nonchalant manner.

I thought he was joking, because he always asked the more experienced girls in the group to sing solos at short notice; only on that particular morning they were out on another job. It was only when I heard Klemperer, in his gruff, broken-English accent, saying, "Mr McCarthy, have you got the soprano?" that I realised it was for real!

Although I was familiar with the melodies of the soprano arias, I had never actually studied them, let alone sung them in German! But once John had escorted me down to the front row, where the distinguished group of soloists was waiting, I had no other option but to get on with the job.

The reason for the sudden replacement was the indisposition of Elizabeth Scharwzkopf, the famous German soprano, who happened to be married to Walter Legge. The other luminaries were the mezzo-soprano Christa Ludwig, the Swedish tenor Nicholai Gedda, the bass Walter Berry, and the English tenor Peter Pears, whose singing of the part of the Evangelist was out of this world. But they were all so charming and encouraging, that I just relaxed, and let the voice speak for itself. I'm sure my German left much to be desired, but I didn't care.

That evening, I suddenly realised that I had just sung a duet with the great Christa Ludwig. Unfortunately, no one with clout, such as Walter Legge, or officials of EMI, were present that day. "What a pity" was born that day. It has followed me throughout my career, even during successful moments. I have never been able to understand the reason for this declamation: perhaps people expect more of me than I am willing, or able, to give. I think I'll have it inscribed on my headstone, along with 'what a waste'.

Working with artists and conductors, such as Benjamin Britten, Otto Klemperer, John Barbirolli and Leonard Bernstein, to name but a few, was part of our daily routine and considered "just another job". With hindsight, I view the situation rather differently. For this reason alone, I was overjoyed when John McCarthy was awarded an OBE for his contribution to music, since his efforts lined our pockets as well.

It was his invitation to join the Ambrosians on a trip to Rome that changed my life. For some time, I had been feeling unsettled. I missed teaching at Roedean, which I had to leave when full-time commitments with the Ambrosians made it impossible to combine both jobs. Moreover, I realised that music wasn't enough for me. I longed to explore new countries and meet new people, away from the world of recording studios and concert halls.

My great friend Morag Durie, whom I had met at college, had gone to Rome to study singing, but abandoned it in favour of a handsome Italian. Wise girl! During our trip, we talked about my fear of stagnation, and the overall need for change. When she suggested going to Rome for a year, I said, "Why not?" Inspired by our decision, I set my plans in motion on my return to London.

To ensure my financial security, I crash-coursed my way through a diploma to teach English to foreigners, which I thoroughly enjoyed. Then I went to Ireland to discuss the challenge with my parents. As always, they gave me their blessing, reassured by the fact that I would still be living in Europe. As it turned out, I spent longer periods at home with them than when I was living in London.

And so, at the end of the swinging sixties, amid sad farewells to colleagues and friends, who thought I was crazy, I set out for Rome on the biggest adventure of my life. Little did I know that sixteen years would pass before I would return to live in the UK.

Chapter 3

Doing What the Romans Do

I loved Rome from the moment I arrived. The very air seemed to be intoxicated with the buzz and excitement generated by the *Dolce Vita* era. Film stars and jet-setters graced the luxury hotels, cafes and restaurants on the fashionable, and expensive, Via Veneto, while sumptuous parties were held on the terraces of luxury apartments and villas.

I used to buy copies of *Stop* and *Oggi*, the tabloid magazines, which kept one up-to-date with the latest gossip about who was in town, and how the other half lived. This included stars from Richard Burton and Elizabeth Taylor, Gregory Peck – my Adonis- Anthony Quinn, Tyrone Power and Linda Christian to Audrey Hepburn, to name but a few. Morag and I used to dress-up in our best clothes to visit the loos of the Excelsior and Hotel de la Ville, in the hope of catching a glimpse of the famous. But we never did.

At that time, the cinema industry was at its peak in Rome. Directors like De Laurentis, Fellini and Pavolini were making legendary films like *Roman Holiday*, *Cleopatra* and *Three Coins in a Fountain*, which afforded the outsider a peep at the beauty of the city; but one has to see Rome for oneself to appreciate its extra ordinary beauty, even when it is raining.

Romans, referred to as *terroni* by their northern Italian counterparts, work and play hard, although their laid-back facade often acts as a camouflage. I got to know them well, through my work, and found them to be kind, caring and great fun. Italians have a great empathy with Ireland, which generated an immediate chemistry between us; in fact, we just clicked.

Everything got off to a flying start from day one, when I got a part-time job in a school teaching English as a foreign language. I had already been initiated into working irregular and long hours through my singing work, so teaching until 10 pm was no problem. Neither was indulging in Italian cuisine and good wine until the early hours, in truly Roman style! And who wouldn't?

Within a few weeks I found a quaint, old-fashioned apartment in the Bohemian quarter of Trastevere, where I taught English and practiced top notes above the noise of the busy streets below. I always think of Trastevere as the Montmartre of Rome. In the early 1970s it was the ideal place for artists, poets, composers and eccentrics, like me.

I lived in a typical cobbled street called Via della Luce (the way of light), where we unashamedly displayed our washing from the windows. We became so familiar with each other's bits and pieces, that when my panties flew off into the breeze, they were nobly retrieved and returned. In the evenings, friends and neighbours would gather outside the local bars and colourful pizzerias to chat and relax, after one's daily work was finished. It was a great way to live, and I was in my element.

It wasn't long until my planned musical sabbatical was aborted. Soon after my arrival, I was invited to dinner by Italian friends of my Belfast teachers, who were the founders of the Belfast Operatic Society. Unhappy with my vocal progress in England, they seized the opportunity, via their Italian conspirators, to arrange a meeting with the well-known Italian baritone Giuseppe Forgione. Once again, my future was being decided by teachers, under whose control I unwittingly remained. It was a "Catch 22" situation; I was caught between my broad-minded parents, who believed in allowing their children to make their own decisions – and thereafter learn from their mistakes – and those who thought they owned my voice. Decades passed before I learnt to trust my own instincts and avoid being dissuaded against my better judgement.

In spite of everything, I enjoyed my singing lessons with Forgione, who was no fool where musicianship and vocal technique were concerned. Not only was he an excellent singer, but an organist and double-bass player as well. Such were his skills that he immediately re-shaped my voice into the original Italian technique with which I had won the scholarship to London. It also enabled me to tackle the Verdi and Puccini repertoire, which I loved.

Through Forgione's influence, it wasn't long before I set off on my first singing engagement, on a memorable train journey, through orange and lemon groves, to a village outside the southern town of Bari, in Puglia. Our open air concert took place in the village square, where, as the pathetic character of Liú in Puccini's *Turandot*, I sang my heart out to real music lovers. Because they were poorer than those further north, and had few operatic treats, their appreciation was limitless. To say that we were acclaimed is an understatement. Our arrival resembled an Oscar night as the fans, ignoring me, screamed out the names of my better-known colleagues, including Forgione. But my big moment came at the end of the evening when I, too, was mobbed, after I had sung the difficult high note at the end of Liú's poignant aria, which Italians just love to hear.

Unfortunately, it was to be both my debut and swan song in Italian romantic opera. Unless one is a big star, Italians are not happy when foreigners perform their repertoire. I agree with them. Not only can the Italian language and passion be more fully expressed by a native Italian, but they have voices and looks to die for. "A package deal" is how one would describe it in the profession. Instead, I was destined to perform music composed in a more modern, *avant garde* idiom.

It is hard to believe that the opportunity to sing this music emerged from a chance meeting on a Roman bus when the Italian conductor and pianist Piero Guarino sat down on the seat next to me while the bus was making its way along the Via del Corso. Piero had impressed us all in the Ambrosians Singers when he conducted *Tongues of Fire*, by the contemporary Greek composer Jani Christou, at the Oxford Bach Festival, the year before I left London. My role as chief wailer must have left an indelible mark on Piero's memory.

"I can't believe it!" he said. "I've been looking for you everywhere. Can you sing a new work for me in three weeks' time?"

Without hesitation I accepted, and the deal was clinched there and then, without my even looking at the score to see if I could sing it. I hadn't long to wait, because the following day I was invited to the Hungarian composer Roman Vlad's lovely home, near the Italian presidential palace, to look over his exciting work *Cinque Elegie su Testi Biblici.* In later years, as well as writing biographies of Benjamin Britten and Stravinsky, he was to become artistic director of La Scala, Milan. In 1999, I met his son Alessio in Genoa, when he invited me to coach Benjamin Britten's *The Rape of Lucretia* at Teatro Carlo Fenice, of which he was artistic director. I was flattered that he remembered me after all those years.

Many people with influence in the world of music were present at my Roman debut in the Teatro Ai Dioscuri that night in April, 1967; it was also near the presidential palace, in the spectacularly floodlit Piazza Quirinale.

That evening, my roller-coaster Italian ride began when I was snapped up by a group of musicians called Nuova Consonanza. These fun-loving people came together to promote intricate, and often impossibly difficult, works by new composers, for which they needed someone like me, with a brass neck, vocal chords of iron, and a taste for adventure. For some of the pieces, it was both the beginning and end in one concert; but many survived my initial renditions, and lived to see another performance. Difficult leaps and gurgles were so demanding that one of my American colleagues, Anne English-Santucci said: "You'd need a degree in engineering to decipher some of the signs you're supposed to sing!" Indeed, I spent so many hours trying to understand "music" written like TV aerials, that I was forced to hunt out the composers from their dens to ask what they meant, and how I was to interpret it.

Few complimented me on the beauty of my singing, but then, it wasn't Mozart. Instead, after each marathon, I was usually greeted by exhausted onlookers gasping: "How did you do it?" One of my long-suffering neighbours said that I sounded like someone in labour! But I didn't care. I was having fun on a mentally stimulating roller with my group, and who wouldn't?

We spent August rehearsing at the fashionable Italian resort of Porto Santo Stefano, because the conductor, Marcello Panni, had rented a villa among the rich and famous. I stayed in the splendid villa of one of my affluent English students, overlooking the harbour. When we weren't sailing and swimming, we spent evenings speaking English on her terrace, while magnificent yachts came and went below.

The actual "getting it into the voice" took place in our front garden in Ireland, until my more classically educated mother could bear it no longer. Putting her head out of a top window, she shouted down: "Couldn't you find an easier way of earning a living?"

The "number" that really did bring down the house at the Venice Biennale that summer of 1970 was a brilliantly illustrated work – in which I was a bird called Bombiillus Garrilus – by the Sicilian composer and painter Francesco Pennisi. Just before the concert was due to start, the ingenious Marcello decided to liven it up by asking the nearby La Fenice theatre to lend us the Papagena bird costume, used in their *Magic Flute* productions. With minutes to spare, I was zipped into a mass of feathers and pushed onto the stage, unaware that there was a huge tail which moved in time with each note I sang. To add to the chaos, a feathered garland had also been draped round my head and over my left eye, obliterating my view of poor Marcello. After a few erratic beats, he looked over to his left – from where the producer had told me not to move – to find two frightened eyes peering out from behind the plumes. Later I was told that there was a queue for the ladies room that night, in a wonderful palazzo on the Grand Canal, to repair make-up damage, after the audience, including many luminaries, had fallen apart with laughter. I shall never live down that evening when Venetian elitist barricades collapsed.

I always kept in touch with my old colleagues from London, who would contact me when they came to Italy on holiday or for work; so when my friend Dorothy Dorow told me that she was going to sing at Rome's Accademia of Santa Cecilia, I was delighted for her. Not only is the Accademia a world-renowned seat of learning, but also a distinguished concert venue. Celebrated artists perform music at the highest level for the well-attended winter subscription concerts and recitals. But the event to which Rome concert-goers were really looking forward in 1970 was the long-awaited, first Italian performance of the *St. Luke*

Passion, by the Polish composer Christof Penderecki.

The posters advertising the three consecutive concerts were already all over Rome when Dorothy rang with the news that she had influenza. There and then I downed tools and sped to her bedside. Not only had she a high fever, but wild ideas.

"Will you do it if I can't, Marge?"

"No," was my emphatic reply, while my own blood pressure rose to match hers. Both of us were used to reading modern music in the Ambrosians; but one glance at the intricate score on her bed convinced me that only a madwoman would undertake such a challenge, let alone attempt such excruciatingly high notes at short notice.

Intricate and specialised contemporary masterpieces, like the Penderecki, are in few singers' repertoire, so that when a performer is indisposed, all hell lets loose until a replacement is found. The only other soprano who knew the work was in Poland, which, because of restrictions imposed by the, then ruling, regime, she couldn't leave. In the hope that Dorothy would recover in time, the concerts were rescheduled to begin three days later. But it wasn't to be. By Saturday night, while Dorothy's condition worsened, the prospect of my stepping into her shoes loomed, despite opposition from the conductor, Jermsky Shemkov.

The following morning, I was having a leisurely Sunday breakfast when the phone rang. It was the Accademia instructing me to go to their impressive concert hall, the Auditorio Via della Concilliazione – within sight of St. Peter's Basilica – to sight-read an unknown work. It was a daunting trial before musicians, expertly equipped to criticise an inexperienced foreign singer. But everyone was so kind and supportive that I relaxed and spent the rest of the day at home learning one of the most exciting works I have ever performed.

In the meantime, while Dorothy's condition, although not serious, showed little sign of improving, I rehearsed in a daze. The day before the first concert, I still didn't know if I should buy a new dress, let alone psychologically prepare myself for such an auspicious occasion. But the suspense came to an end, when later that morning, the governing body of the Accademia arrived to sit

34

down, in the role of a jury, in the stalls. Only then did I realise that it was make or break time for me.

"What shall I do?" I said, in a panic, to my bass colleague sitting beside me.

"Just keep calm, and continue as you've been doing."

Naturally, one couldn't expect the Accademia to engage an unheard-of singer without an audition. But they did. Not only did it herald a new career for me as an international soloist, but a happy future collaboration with the Accademia. Dorothy sent me a lovely bouquet, which was presented to me on stage. She had considered a plant, but, knowing me, was afraid I'd drop it on my toes!

Until this remarkable opportunity, I had been, and still am on home soil, regarded as a misplaced singer and musician, for whom, according to another soprano, "the wheel of fortune never turned". Over the years, I had accepted my underdog role, and found other things in life which are just as important as music. Therefore, it never occurred to me that Cinderella's luck might change. But it did. Italians accepted me on merit and at face value, and not on whom I knew. And so, when I signed a contract with one of the world's most distinguished concert societies at an undreamt-of fee, I felt that my musical bridesmaid days had been left behind in Ireland and the UK. Not only was it the beginning of a lifelong musical liaison with the nicest people one would hope to meet, but a change of lifestyle, which I wouldn't have missed for the world, although it was some time before the seeds sewn that evening in Via della Concilliazione bore fruit.

In the meantime, I became known as the "singing fire brigade", after news of my rescue of indisposed, or deposed, singers rapidly spread round the profession. On one mission, I had to call upon Rome's public services, after I survived what must be every singer's nightmare: not being able to turn up!

At the time of this traumatic experience, I was living near the lovely Piazza Venezia, in the heart of Rome, where, in the early 1940s, Mussolini delivered his historic orations from a balcony overlooking the square. I was imagining the verbal, and legal, abuse I would get from the RAI – the Italian radio and TV network – which had begged me to rescue a concert after a soprano had "chickened out".

Because the live transmission was at their concert hall at Foro Italico, beside the famous football stadium on the other side of the city, I decided to make an early start and phone for a taxi; but there weren't any. In sheer panic, I ran to the square, in the hope of catching a passing one, only to discover that they, too, were but a dream. It was then that I made a mad dash towards a sign displaying, *Vigili Notturni*, meaning "night vigilantes" in Italian, with my evening dress over my arm. To my horror, I was informed that traffic throughout the city had come to a standstill, including buses and taxis. Nothing appeals to the Italian male like a damsel in distress. And so, with sirens blaring, they pushed me into a car and got me to the hall, with minutes to spare. My Formula One-type arrival, after a mad drive through side streets, might have caused quite a stir to those who also managed to arrive, but it was music to nerves of the conductor, Feruccio Scaglia, who was becoming increasingly concerned about my absence.

"I don't know the piece!" I wailed.

"But I do," he assured me.

While I sipped a brandy, we devised emergency plans, in case I got lost. But there was no need, because the conductor was in such command of the situation, that I just relaxed and let the voice take over. After the concert he said: "You should do that more often, Marjorie. I've never heard you sing better." We decided that because I was so calm, I must have left my nerves behind in Piazza Venezia.

I had temporarily moved near there, and within walking distance of the Trevi Fountain, after a number of incidents forced me to leave Via della Luce. It was a pity, even if my Bohemian flat in Trastevere was considered entirely unsuitable for a prima donna to live in. To me, its rather down trodden atmosphere was the ideal setting in which to sing, and play Puccini's wonderful operas. It was during one of these rapturous and poignant sessions, while accompanying myself at the piano in one of Mimi's heart-rending moments from *La Bohème*, that an extraordinary incident occurred.

The prelude to this story really began when my downstairs neighbour paid me an unexpected visit to discuss a rather delicate matter. To our mutual consternation, it appeared that if we simultaneously sat on our respective loos – hers was directly below mine – she got more than she bargained for if I pulled my chain before she had completed her "business". After a lengthy, but amicable, discussion, it was agreed that her son would call on me to further discuss the plumbing crisis.

Next morning, my journey into Mimi's tragic world was interrupted by a ring at the door. When I opened it, there was a handsome stranger gazing at me with awe-struck eyes. Without thinking – remember that I was a foreign girl living alone – I slammed the door in his face! Only then did I remember "the lavatory man", as he became known. He had such Italian good looks that I couldn't believe that I had missed out on a hunk of a Puccini hero, downstairs, right under my nose. He was still standing there when I reopened the door, through which I immediately pulled him towards the separate loo. There I delivered a long lecture on its misbehaviour.

"Your poor mother," I said. "She must dread going to the bathroom." He must have thought I was mad – I found out later that he did – because, when I carried on about my lavatorial dilemma, he abruptly changed the subject. Finally, in desperation, I said: "Haven't you come about your mother's toilet?"

"No, Signorina," he replied. "When I heard this heavenly sound from my favourite opera floating out from your house, I had to see where it was coming from!"

The story spread like wildfire, since the young man's girlfriend and I studied with the same teacher! As you can imagine, the story lost nothing in the telling, for by the time his version was added, the original was nearly unrecognisable

One morning, my dream of being offered a singing engagement on my own merit, and not as a substitute, came true. You can imagine my surprise when a telegram arrived from La Fenice, Venice, that most beloved of opera houses, inviting me to sing a work by a young German composer, who had reached the finals of the coveted Marzotto Prize, donated by the Italian textile firm of that name.

The American tenor Herbert Handt was rehearsing at La Fenice when they were looking for a soprano with perfect pitch and the ability to learn quickly, as time was short, to perform the demanding role of a crazy demigoddess, based on Buchner's *Leonce und Lena*. When Herbert was asked if he could recommend a soprano, he remembered my rescue mission at Santa Cecilia. He said: "Perhaps Wright could do it." Bless him.

With three weeks to learn the piece – a lifetime for me – I had time to have some new clothes made. It was then that I realised that singing, for which one must be elegantly dressed, is an expensive occupation; even outfits which would normally be used for special occasions become one's working clothes. Competing with Italians who, to begin with, are endowed with good looks and beautiful hair, is a daunting task. But when a friend introduced me to her wizard dressmaker, who didn't even need a pattern, a vision, beyond all expectations, emerged out of nothing. Travelling expenses often have to come out of the artist's own pocket, while hotel and restaurant bills quickly mount up. There is also the cost of singing lessons, which, in my case, were often a waste of time, because my unorthodox music was out of the tutor's depth. It was almost out of mine, too!

I fell madly in love with Venice. Who wouldn't? My visit was the first of many to this paradise, built on a lagoon, from which cars are banned; the only means of transport is by water, or on foot.

Over the years, the quaint, old-fashioned Albergo La Fenice, practically next door to the opera house, where visiting artistes stay, became a second home to me. The staff themselves could have graced any theatrical establishment. During his stay there, Ingmar Bergman, the Swedish film director, snapped up one of the receptionists to play the part of the butler in one of his productions. How those wonderful people coped with the histrionics of demanding performers, like me, was beyond belief; but they did.

The theatre itself, with its plum and gold decor, had such a warm and embracing atmosphere that I rarely felt nervous performing there. Those who grew to love it were devastated when it was destroyed by fire in 1996. It was a harrowing experience watching, on TV, all those precious memories going up in smoke. It has risen again, like the phoenix after which it is named. But for me, it will not be the Fenice I knew.

We didn't win that year's Marzotto Prize; we were pipped at the post by the French composer Marius Constant, whose work was sung by the great French diva Regine Créspin. As a young novice, I was in awe of such a huge star; but she was charming and without airs and graces that less successful singers assume. The competition itself was held at Valdagno, not far from Venice. After the concert, we were invited to a reception at the magnificent Marzotto family villa, along with the other participants, who included Natalie Ginsburg, the winner of that year's Marzotto Prize for literature.

At the end of the evening, we had to rejoin our Venice-bound coach at the local hotel, where journalists were phoning news of the winners back to base. When I asked an elderly man if he knew the whereabouts of our coach, he didn't hear me. Eventually, as I shouted above the din, he said: "You must excuse me, I'm rather deaf." He then informed me that he was the arts critic for a Roman newspaper. I couldn't have made much impression on him, for he neither recognised nor congratulated me on my vocal gymnastics.

Although we didn't win, we were invited back to La Fenice two months later as part of the Venice Biennale. It was the beginning of my long love affair with La Fenice and Venice.

Chapter 4

Branching Out

My past continued to pave the way to my future when Piero
Guarino recommended me to Jani Christou, the Greek composer
through whom we first met, to sing the part of Clytemnestra in his
new opera, based on the *Agememnon.*

Once the deal had been clinched over the phone, Christou
and I decided to meet in Greece the following January when,
having assessed my voice and dramatic ability, he would put the
finishing touches to the opera, before embarking on a world tour
stretching from England, Greece, Denmark, to Japan and beyond.

As the New Year came and went, the promised plane ticket
never arrived. In Athens the phone at the Christou home
remained unanswered. Then, one evening, the mystery was finally
solved. By an extraordinary stroke of fate, the mezzo-soprano wife
of Christou's publisher, who had just arrived in Rome to perform
at the Filarmonica, succumbed to a sore throat. When she rang to
ask me to deputise for her, I told her that I could undertake no
further commitment until I knew what was happening in Greece.
After an ominous silence, she asked me to meet her at her apartment. Judging by the tone of her voice, I had already guessed that
something was terribly wrong. Over a glass of brandy she told me
the terrible news: Christou and his wife had both been killed in a
car crash in Athens and, since the opera was unfinished, the world
tour had been cancelled. It was a dreadful career blow to me, but
nothing compared to the personal loss suffered by the Christou
family. After we had all come to terms with the tragedy, it tran-

spired that it had been just assumed that everyone knew about it.

In the early 1970s I was on a musical high in Dublin, a city full of literary and musical culture which I adore. The Irish radio station RTÉ had given me my early chances in broadcasting and recorded wonderful moments, like the annual performance of Handel's *Messiah* with the well-known Our Lady's Choral Society which, in those days, was held in the National Stadium, generally used for boxing contests and complete with turnstiles. I shall not forget one performance of this work, when the smoke from the previous "rounds" got to work on my throat, already suffering from the effects of a cold. As my condition deteriorated, I had to pull out all my emergency stops to combat the coughing and spluttering which plagued me right up to the interval. Some of the sympathetic audience eased my suffering when they arrived backstage with gifts of Vick and cough sweets. They certainly did the trick, helping me to reach the last top note in *I Know that My Redeemer Liveth*, in which I gave my all.

Sadly, my happy time was brought to an abrupt halt when Dublin's most illustrious and influential music critic, wrote a damaging criticism of me in Ireland's most widely read newspaper, after I had sung in Dvorák's *Requiem* at a public concert for RTÉ. In it he said that after hearing me sing in three recent concerts, any mistakes made that evening were not "accidents of the night". Catastrophically for me, it ended my career in Ireland, because the elite musical hierarchy believed him, while those who would have liked to employ me feared the wrath of his pen.

Some months later, while compiling a CV, I came upon the paper's write-ups of the concerts. To my amazement, I discovered that name of this damaging critic was only at the bottom of one, while the other two had been written by his wife – to whom I had actually spoken on the evening she deputised for him – and another unfamiliar name. It is not the first time that an "absentee" critic has used his pen to such scathing effect. Unfortunately, there are many music critics who are disappointed performers with limited personal experience of what it is like to perform in public, and therefore have little insight into what makes an artist tick. On the other hand, there are those so endowed with understanding and knowledge that it is wise to listen to them, since they are usually right. I discovered this some years later, when a knowledgeable successor to the above mentioned reviewed a recital of Schoenberg and Berg, which I performed at the Belfast Festival at Queens. In it he wrote that I was a contralto, and not a mezzo-soprano. How I regretted not following his opinion sooner; but at that stage I was only too relieved to be a mezzo-soprano, after singing for decades as a soprano. All very confusing to those who are not familiar with "the voice".

I shall never forget a public letter written by the composer Seán Ó Riada to the critic who didn't like me in which he said that he would worry if he ever gave him a good write-up! And so, I certainly wasn't the only home-grown artist who suffered at the hand of this man who forced us to look beyond Irish musical circles and seek work abroad. With hindsight, he did us all a favour since we all successfully spread our wings on the international circuit.

My fondest Irish musical memories rest with my friend, the late Father Seamus Moore, who was so prematurely taken from us, after devoting himself to the pastoral and artistic needs of the people of Newry. Father Seamus's talent for concert promotion, combined with vast musical knowledge, was boundless. Those of us who were privileged to take part in his "Singing For Joy" concerts still talk about those happy times.

I never managed to live down the evening when I took off my evening shoes, only to find that I couldn't get them back onto my swollen feet. Eventually, after a lot of pushing and shoving by a mighty band of helpers, I was reunited with them, just in time to sing the duet scene from *La Bohème*, in which the tenor held me to his chest in such a tight embrace that I could hardly find enough breathing space to reach the exposed top note at the end of the duet. The Warrenpoint participants, including myself, nearly didn't arrive at that concert, because Father Moore was so busy organising the arrival of the Bishop that he forgot to send transport to collect us. I began to worry, until my mother said: "They can't start without you." Eventually, our chauffeur did arrive to take us, at breakneck speed, to the hall where Father Moore, baton in hand, was standing on the steps in his cassock, shouting: "Hurry up, hurry up, the Bishop is waiting." When we missed a beat in one aria, Father Moore was so anxious about the Bishop's reaction that he mouthed up to me on stage: "Do you think the Bishop noticed?" I'm sure he didn't, since I later found out that His Lordship was tone deaf, and more likely to have been indulging in a quiet nap.

The concert to top all concerts was when Belfast Philharmonic Society, to celebrate its centenary in 1974, took Beethoven's *Ninth Symphony* to Newry, organised by Father Moore himself. To the best of my knowledge, it was the first time this long work had been aired in Newry, a town used to Handel's *Messiah* and Haydn's *Creation*, with good tunes and solos. Unfortunately, there is a long sit, through three orchestral movements, until a quartet of soloists leads the way, the only one having anything like a solo part being the bass.

When Father Moore heard that I was going to sing in such an important concert, he immediately mounted a publicity campaign for the "local girl". Somehow, the only photograph of me he could find was in my school uniform, which appeared on the front page of the *Newry Reporter* under the headline "Come and Hear Your Own", to which the town enthusiastically responded.

Our contribution had been scheduled for the second half of the programme, so that my colleagues and I arrived from Belfast in time for what we imagined would be the interval. When we reached the church where, at the height of the Troubles, the concert was being held, the Welsh conductor Alun Francis, at that time in charge of the Ulster Orchestra, was standing outside the front door.

"Is this the interval?" we enquired.

"No, we haven't even started yet. They're too busy trying to get Marjorie's fans seated!"

Eventually, after extra chairs were found, the concert got under way. Performing to a home audience is a daunting experience, but when we took our seats on the platform, I was confronted by a sea of familiar faces – all blissfully unaware of the length of the work and the brevity of my contribution – waiting for "their own" to do them proud. After their disappointing ordeal, I was faced with a throng of frustrated protestors backstage. "You didn't even sing a solo. You'd have thought they'd have given you one in your own home-town."

Beethoven was lucky that he wasn't exhumed that evening. One gentleman, in true Glyndebourne fashion, had even brought a picnic, which he and his groups of fans hadn't been able to eat.

On another visit to Ulster, I had the great pleasure of singing with the tenor James Johnston – one of the province's greatest exports – in a performance of Mendelssohn's beautiful oratorio *Elijah*, in Londonderry's lovely Guildhall. At that time Jimmy had forsaken the field of opera for his successful butcher's business in Belfast, only leaving it to sing when he felt like it. At our final rehearsal, when he hadn't appeared, panic ensued, while those in charge made a hasty retreat to, I assume, ring around for a replacement. In his absence, the continuo-player still went ahead and struck up the chord of the recitative to the lovely tenor aria *If With All Your Heart*, with Jimmy's voice entering, dead on time, to synchronise with his arrival at the door of the Guildhall. Then, accompanied by the orchestra, as he walked up the imposing marble staircase of that magnificent building, his glorious sounds made us believe that we had already gone to heaven. By the time he took his seat beside me on the platform, we were soon brought back to normal when, in his down-to-earth Belfast way, Jimmy turned to me and said, "How are you doin', daughter?"

I often wondered if, with Jimmy's reputation for not turning up, the organisers had arranged a stand-by for him; but that evening, he certainly honoured us with his presence.

On my return to Rome, I faced the horrific experience, with dramatic consequences, of being robbed. I had just returned from signing a contract at the Italian radio, for which I had borrowed a friend's mink cravat. Italian fashion is legendary, and in winter fur coats, the like of which I have not seen since or before, are brought out to display opulence, an act better known as *bella figura* in Italy. Therefore, it was essential that I too should sport a prosperous aura. Of course the radio didn't know that on that unforgettable afternoon I had to cancel English students. To them, I was the successful prima donna. But the burglars knew that I went out every afternoon at a certain time; only on that particular one, they didn't bargain for my change of schedule and return home. As I went towards the bedroom, one of the intruders ran towards me, closely followed by two others making a quick get-away. When one of them caught sight of my piece of mink, he tried to grab it from my throat; but by the time my almighty scream sent them scuttling down the stairs, they had already slipped through the ranks of a huge crowd of locals, alerted by my cries for help

"Didn't you catch them?" I wailed.

"No, Signorina, we thought you were practicing!"

It so happened that the aborted robbery had taken place a short time after my mad goddess performance in Venice, so inevitably, the crowd found it impossible to distinguish between my cries for help and the excruciatingly high notes I had been attempting to reach.

Unfortunately, the thieves did manage to get away with my mother's engagement ring and I was devastated. The next day, after the local rag announced "Irish singer disturbs thieves who were forced to leave behind furs and jewels", I had no option but to leave Via della Luce for my temporary accommodation near Piazza Venezia, since I suspected that many of the locals were involved in the break-in.

I lost my voice as a result of this terrifying incident, just as I was due to leave Rome to record a programme of Italian operatic arias for Ulster Television. My ailing father was thrilled when he heard about the Christmas Eve transmission, for which I joined him at an impromptu party at the nursing home where the Alexian brothers took such loving care of him.

Somehow, the burglary story had been leaked to the press, and when I arrived at my Belfast hotel, an enthusiastic photographer was waiting for me. He had found an old-fashioned organ, with a stool, upon which I was ordered to sit. The following evening, an unflattering photograph of me, my arms spread out over the keyboard, was published in the widely read *Belfast Telegraph* under the headline: "Ulster Singer After A Trying Weekend."

Shortly after this episode, BBC Northern Ireland arrived in Rome to make a documentary on Irish people living there. Naturally, I was still suffering from the after-effects of the robbery, so that when the programme researcher arrived at my new apartment, I was only too willing to tell all. Only then did I see the funny side of it, when he and the rest of the home team started laughing at the thought of my cries for help being mistaken for my "singing". We had a wonderful time filming in my friend's garden, especially adorned for the occasion with false roses, which had been delicately pinned onto the hedge. Unfortunately, I collided with the hedge as I "casually" strolled down the path, explaining why I had come to Rome in the first place. It was my first recorded interview on television; to say that I was terrified is an understatement. Under such pressure I was sure that my stammer would return, but I forgot all about it when Sean Rafferty and I began the first of many amusing interviews for BBC Northern Ireland. During our chat I told him that my Italian singing career began when I met a conductor on a bus. He remembered this when previewing the eventual transmission of the documentary from Belfast, inviting the province to tune in that evening to hear "how a singer from Warrenpoint had met a conductor on a Roman bus"! By lunchtime news had spread round the town like wild-fire, for who else could it be but "their own"? Next morning, my mother was besieged with people congratulating her on my engagement to a bus conductor!

Filming was at its peak when In lived in Rome, and extras were in constant demand. I willingly joined this happy crowd after a friend mentioned my name to a Rome-based American film agent, who was casting for a film *The Statue*, starring David Niven and Verna Lisi. In response to his call, I unexpectedly found myself queuing up with starry-eyed ambitious talent waiting to be interviewed for what might be our break into the big time.

Since I seldom had success at musical auditions, I didn't rate my chances with film ones, but once I was seated before three formidable film moguls, I decided to let my hair down and go for it. The one who did most of the talking was the director, Rod Amato, who aroused my interest when he turned round to his colleagues and said: "Don't you think she's a little young for David Niven's housekeeper?" I gasped in belief: to serve my idol would have been too much to hope for.

"Can't you pad me up and *make* me look older?" I pleaded, while consoling myself with the knowledge that at least I was still young and not past my sell-by date. Suddenly, the news that there was a possibility of appearing in a film with David Niven had given me a taste for the big screen. Even when Rod Amato said, "What are you like before a camera", I nonchalantly answered, "Just as I am before a TV camera". Little did he know that I nurtured a secret fear of TV cameras and microphones. Amato had asked me to bring photographs of myself in a bikini to his apartment by noon the following day. I had forgotten all about it until he rang me to ask where they were. In a panic, I searched for some taken on holiday in Greece, but to no avail. Then, as a last resort, I phoned an American photographer friend who rushed over to my flat and took, in the freezing temperatures of mid-February, some very flattering poses. They certainly did the trick, for, a week later, my agent rang with the news that I had got the tiny part of a "rather dubious woman" in an extract of the musical *Hair*, which was to be used in the film. I nearly had to be resuscitated when I was handed a work permit classing me as a stripper! Apparently, the musical had a scene in which disrobing was featured.

To avoid discovery, I immediately set to work on a plan of disguise and secrecy, since I hadn't told a living soul about my "double life". They wouldn't have understood that I needed money to further my "other", more expensive career. I was confident that my master plan was infallible, timing the disrobing scene to perfection so that I was left with more, rather than less on my person, just like my bikini photos. But alas, a male Irish friend, who lived in Rome, found out and rang me up in a state of panic.

"Are you mad?" he shrieked. "Go out and buy a copy of the *Daily American* and you'll find a photograph of yourself, half-naked, beside David Niven in his shirt-tails." I nearly had a heart-attack, since we were both singers and knew the devastating effect this deviation from the elite musical world could have on my career if news of my cavorting round in such unseemly circumstances got out. Fortunately, I got away with it until, years later, my secret was more widely revealed when the BBC included the film in its Christmas programme. Many cards arrived from the UK reporting a "Marge look-a-like" on the telly, while those who had been at school, or shared a flat with me in London knew that the crazy woman in the film was the real me.

Two minor film appearances followed, both under the direction of the famous Billy Wilder. In the first one, *Avanti*, I was an over-protective mother shielding her son from the strangely clad Jack Lemmon. Alas, when I took a group of friends to see the completed film, my scene had been cut out! The second, *Identikit*, was with the lovely Elizabeth Taylor, whose famous violet eyes were even more beautiful in reality. For this film, Billy Wilder picked me from a crowd of extras at dawn – filming starts early – to portray an over-dressed American tourist in a white pleated skirt, frilly blouse, and a hat made of tulle with a rose plonked on the crown. I looked, and felt, ridiculous, on a sweltering mid-August day, especially when I had to answer a desperate call of nature and visit a cafe. One of my pals said that the picture of me forcing my way to the loo through a throng of mesmerised Italians should have been incorporated into the film.

Sadly, my film adventures came to an end when I had to choose between singing and being funny, after I was invited to appear nude in a film starring Marcello Mastroianni and Vittorio Gassman, the two machos of the Italian cinema. Since it was to be premiered at the Venice Festival – in the presence of luminaries before whom I was going to sing two weeks later – my friends and I decided that, considering that I was no Brigitte Bardot or Sophia Loren, I should concentrate on my "real career", which was about to blossom.

Before I settled down, I was offered innumerable and lucrative jobs as a tourist guide which, in the intense heat of summer, I thoroughly enjoyed. I met the most unusual and misinformed groups of tourists; one, while viewing the famous "wedding cake" in Piazza Venezia, built in 1911, with the tomb of the unknown soldier added in 1921, suddenly asked me: "Was that built before or after Romulus and Remus?" It wasn't funny when an erudite American professor asked me to explain the unification of Italy to his family, which I avoided by explaining that it wasn't in the itinerary!

In international cities, like Rome, Paris and New York, it is inevitable that one meets famous people. One evening I was rescued by a "prince" from an unpleasant head-on collision with a very nasty French conductor. As usual, I had been summoned to save a last-minute situation, for which a liaison with the conductor was imperative. When I approached him during a coffee break to discuss work to be performed – Stravinsky's superb arrangement of three Hugo Wolf Spanish songs – he refused to lift his head from a copy of the French newspaper *Le Monde*. If the chemistry between performer and conductor is missing all hell can let loose, creating a nerve-racking experience for all concerned, which is exactly what happened when I faced this arrogant man, ready for battle, across the stage of Rome's Teatro Olimpico.

With hindsight, I assumed that the conductor just hated the piece, and couldn't wait to get it over and done with. His speeds were so erratic that the performance developed into a wrestling match, of which the audience was blissfully unaware. Suddenly, in the midst of all the chaos, I heard the voice of the orchestral leader, Angelo Stefanato, beside me whispering: "You set the pace, Marjorie, and we'll follow you." Realising that the orchestra was also suffering got my adrenaline flowing, and once we applied the brakes, we settled down to deliver the passionate and musical rendition of which the music was worthy, with no one being any the wiser except the conductor. To say that he went berserk is an understatement. Professionally speaking, we didn't blame him, for we had wrongly challenged his authority in an "every man for himself" situation, with the soloist and orchestra in the driving seat. At the end of the performance, while war waged backstage, our interpretation drew rapturous applause from both audience and critics. Meanwhile, between numerous trips onto the stage to acknowledge the applause, the conductor verbally attacked me in front of anyone within earshot, including another female colleague, who allowed him to finish his Marjorie character assassination, before stoically defending our friendship. It was then that my knight in shining armour appeared in the shape of the film star Edmund Purdom, who rose to fame in the film *The Student Prince*. Oblivious of the frosty atmosphere around him, he complimented me on the beauty of my singing, which he had recorded, hiding under the stage. It just goes to show that you never know who's listening!

You never knew who you were going to meet either. Professional singers are treated like royalty in Italy so, I was frequently invited to dinner parties and receptions at embassies and glittering occasions. It took some time for me to discover that I was really invited to relieve awkward silences with my funny stories. In both capacities I was invited to a dinner party at the palatial British Council in Rome, in 1972, to honour the seventieth birthday party of the acclaimed British composer Sir William Walton. Jack Buckley, the music consultant of the Council at that time, happened to be, and still is, a good friend of mine. It was through his thoughtfulness that I took my place in the impressive line of dignitaries, including Sir Ashley Clarke, a former British Ambassador, and the author of *A Clockwork Orange*, Anthony Burgess. Jack used to refer to me as the "Duchess of Belfast", which he mischievously wrote on my invitation. Naturally, I was rather overawed in such distinguished company, as we lined up to be introduced; even more so when the toastmaster took my invitation card and announced: "Her Grace, the Duchess of Belfast", in the glory of which I sailed into the reception room, while those with real titles looked on in wonder.

In Italy fellow artists and musicians were very benevolent to each other, a trait which is unique in a cut-throat profession. And so, when my American colleague, Carol Plantamura, heard that the famous German avant-garde composer Karl Heinz Stockhausen was looking for a soprano to perform one of his works on tour she urged me to waste no time getting in touch with him. To be honest, I was more excited about the prospect of meeting one of the world's great contemporary composers than getting the job. And so, having contacted the great man, I set off for Cologne the following Sunday morning. Because there was no direct flight that particular day I flew to Lausanne, from where I caught a connection to Cologne. Herr Stockhausen had told me to ring him on my arrival for directions on how to reach his home, situated in the woods, outside the lovely cathedral city of Cologne, in the spectacular Rhine valley. As the taxi took me through magnificent forests, basking in glorious Autumnal colours, I couldn't help comparing them to my native Ireland, with its similar change of seasons. Beautiful as Italy is, one seems to pass from summer into winter, skipping spring and summer. As we approached the composer's home, set in solitary surroundings and designed by Herr Stockhausen himself, I could see him standing on the lawn waiting to greet me. As I got out of the Mercedes Benz I couldn't believe that I was about to shake the hand of this middle-aged tall and imposing man, with shoulder-length blond hair, who could possibly make or break my career if I were to sing his work.

Before setting out on this daunting encounter, I spent Saturday unsuccessfully scouring Rome for a score of *Momente* – Stockhausen's work for soprano soloist, three choirs and thirteen instruments – for which I was to audition. With a plane to catch the following morning I had no other option than to sight-read the work in question. A normal artist arrives at an audition prepared, and considerable knowledge of the work in question, so how I had the nerve to face a luminary of world renown without a sheet of music beggars belief. But, after the initial shock, Herr Stockhausen was most charming, putting me at my ease as we sat in his study, where so many of his finest works had been composed, discussing the work and its conception. After we had finished, I was invited to stay for dinner with the Stockhausen family, before being driven back to Cologne to say with friends.

Momente had originally been written for the American singer Martina Arroya, who was unable to go on that particular tour. That evening, as I took leave of the Stockhausens, Karlheinz said that if he didn't find the type of singer for whom the work was intended, he would consider me for the part and change the text. But he did, and our paths didn't cross again. When I returned to Italy I was casually telling Franco Donatoni, Stockhausen's maverick Italian counterpart, that I had asked him to demonstrate some of *Momente* for me, he shrieked, "You what? You had the nerve to ask a composer to sing his own work?" In those days I naively believed that if composers wrote for a singer they should be able to sing it themselves.

Like so many frustrated singers, I did the rounds of teachers, searching for, at least, one who might solve our vocal problems. Through friends I was advised to go to Maestra Debora Fambri, an aristocratic lady of grand stature who, with her fascinating Venetian accent and dazzling smile, sat with a shawl around her shoulders administering the art of *bel canto* to her flock.

This grand old lady, who was approaching eighty when I first met her, held an annual birthday party at which her faithful students performed, providing an opportunity for them to display the progress they had made in the interim year. The Maestra didn't believe in pushing a voice beyond its potential, even if it meant taking years to achieve; so you can imagine her reaction when I introduced her to the world of modern vocal gymnastics, the like of which she had never encountered in her long teaching career. Considerably helped by playing the violin earlier on in her life – she rather enjoyed the challenge and became one of the few teachers who was able to help me over almost impossible hurdles. Unfortunately, I was in such a hurry to resolve them that I did not totally benefit from what this wonderful teacher had to contribute; yet, her magic spell produced a more dulcet tone to ease the strain on my neighbours, who considered the sounds emanating from my apartment to be rather strange, to say the least!

As is so often the case with teacher/student relationships, much of the technique learnt from the Maestra took effect in later years, providing invaluable material for my own singing manual. Not one of the Maestra's flock would have considered leaving her, but she realised, in her own unselfish way, that I was a born wanderer and explorer, ready to investigate other ways which might achieve more immediate results.

We never lost touch, so that when her regular accompanist fell ill, she asked me to play at her lessons. I immediately said, "Maestra, you must be desperate, but if you can put up with my vamping, I'd be delighted to help you out." It was also a golden opportunity to see her again and chat about food, since the Maestra was especially partial to bacon and sausages I used to bring her from Ireland, along with other ingredients of an 'Ulster Fry', which she relished. We spent a wonderful week together in which I learnt more listening to her teaching others than when we were on a one-to-one basis. we decided to study the role of Puccini's *Turandot* on her return from her summer holiday; but it was not to be, because the Maestra died peacefully during her annual trip to the sea.

When I used to drive along Italian roads I never ceased to admire the wonderful hillside villages and towns along the way. At night they are especially captivating when shimmering lights portray an atmosphere on homely tranquillity. "How do the people live up there? What do they do all day packed into such a small community?" were just some of the questions I would ask myself. I soon found out when I was invited to sing at the Festival of Two Worlds, held in the lovely town of Spoleto, perched on the side of an Umbrian Hill. I spent nearly three weeks there rehearsing and performing *Laborintus,* by the eminent Italian composer Lucian Berio, involving three female singers, the American soprano Carol Plantamura, the famous American-Armenian mezzo-soprano Cathy Berberian, and yours truly.

The name of the festival, created by the Italian composer Giancarlo Menotti, was derived from the two worlds of Italy and America, from which the majority of the artists were chosen to perform. I had little experience of resident summer festivals, having paid only brief visits to Aldeburgh, in Suffolk, and Edinburgh during my days with the Ambrosian Singers, so I looked forward to this "paid holiday" mingling in idyllic surroundings with top international soloists.

In the intense heat of July, Carol and I, laden with suitcases full of music, left Rome for Spoleto. When we arrived, exhausted and forlorn at the festival office we were informed that there was no accommodation for us; apparently, they had just forgotten about us. Eventually, after what seemed an interminable search, a house was found for us at the foot of a long hill, towards which we made our weary way. Our delight at finding a cul-de-sac house all to ourselves was somewhat short-lived when we discovered that we were not the only occupants. Insects of varying species, including beetles and cockroaches played happily in the concrete floored kitchen.

Carol made herself at home on the first floor, while I chose the pretty bedroom next to the communal bathroom and loo. I congratulated myself at bagging "the penthouse" until I discovered that the only way to obtain hot water was by lighting a fire in a stove in the bathroom, right next to my bedroom! The thought of the temperature inside, when outside it was well over 90 degrees, didn't bear thinking about. Our leisure time was spent out in the woods gathering fuel to heat water to wash our tired feet after struggling up the hill to shop and collect mail. Then, after the descent had been completed, we would again have to brave the ascent to go to rehearsals and concerts. We soon became familiar figures among festival enthusiasts because, bored to tears and left to our devices, Carol and I would sit on walls round the hillside town singing madrigals and musical rounds. Although everyone was very cordial, few were anxious to accept our hospitality or visit 'mates' in our rather isolated house opposite a garage, which resounded like an amphitheatre from dawn to dusk.

There was an unforgettable scenario on our final day in Spoleto when our landlady, whom we hadn't seen from day one, arrived to collect the rent. Not only did she resemble the gipsy Carmen, from Bizet's opera, but she displayed the same fiery temperament when we refused to pay the entire rent, after enduring three weeks in the "House from Hell". Carol attacked first, reaching vocal heights with precision and clarity, while I boomed my disapproval in my more fruity tones.

"Thank you, Signorina", said the enraged woman, "at least you have a lower voice".

The volume of our screaming and shouting even attracted the garage workers, who added their voices to our angry chorus. They knew only too well how festival landlords could unmercifully fleece their victims. But the thing is that, after we had packed our bags and fled, neither Carol nor I can remember paying the bill; in fact, I don't believe we did.

One of my greatest pleasures in life is to listen to elderly peers reminiscing about their distinguished careers. My friends and I used to sit for hours mesmerised by our friend Nunu Sanchioni's dramatically narrating anecdotes. How were we to know that we, too, would become involved in Nun's final act? Apart from the prima donna herself, the principal characters in this unbelievable story were myself and my compatriot, the tenor Bill Mckinney.

Nunu was born in Cairo in 1908, where her father was the Italian Consul. She spent her formative years in Holland, where she performed in the main opera houses. Considered to be the finest coloratura soprano of her generation, Nunu was acclaimed as Adele in Max Rheinhart's 1932 production of *Die Fledermaus* at La Scala, Milan. Unfortunately, ill health, the outbreak of the Second World War and a disastrous marriage to a German aborted Nunu's career, forcing her to return to Rome where we spent many evenings listening to her showing us how to sing top notes in her tiny flat beside the Roman Forum, which she shared with her terrier dog. While on a professional singing engagement in Germany, Bill Mckinney managed to track down the whereabouts of the late husband, whose demise entitled his widow, who retained her German passport, to a pension.

While we were in her company it was impossible not to notice the selection of decorative scarves which Nunu wore round her neck to conceal a growth which, with her improved financial position, combined with our love and support, she decided to have removed. Encouraged by the success of the operation, Nunu decided to undergo a further one to relieve a hernia condition. Since our group of friends became her family, a rota system was set up, with Bill and his pals visiting the hospital during the week, while I was assigned to weekend duty.

On the Saturday after her operation, I found Nunu clearly unwell, and in a distressed condition. Realising that she was nearing her end, she was most anxious that I should help her put her affairs in order. Convinced that it was a combination of post-operative stress and artistic temperament, I ignored her wishes and told her not to talk such nonsense when she was on the brink of starting a new life, with good health to enjoy it. Regrettably, I also ignored her attempts to retrieve a bag of money hidden under her bed, which I assumed was for the upkeep of her dog, that we had already installed in a temporary and loving home. We shall never know, because it was the last time I spoke to Nunu, or saw the money again.

No one could be found on that unforgettable weekend. Our doctor friend was on duty at the Clinica dei Gemelli, where Pope John Paul II was a patient, while Bill was singing in far-off Sardegna. Realising that I was the only one the hospital could contact, I left them my phone number. The following morning I got an early morning call from the hospital with the news that Nunu's condition had suddenly deteriorated. When I got there, I found her in the intensive unit, unable to move because of the tubes and equipment surrounding her, yet desperate to communicate with me. Then later that day I was recalled to the hospital, where not only Nunu, but all the other patients whom I had seen that morning had disappeared from the intensive care unit! Apparently, in the interim period, they had all died and been subsequently removed to the morgue, to where I was escorted to identify Nunu's body.

I had heard far-fetched stories of Italian funerals, but nunu's outshone them all. The drama began after two mortuary attendants informed me that Nunu was to be buried the following Wednesday in a pauper's grave, with only the sign of the cross being made over the coffin. I was then handed the clothes of a Mrs Moscha – the Italian translation is Mrs Fly – which were neither the size or taste of my late friend. After it became obvious that they had got the wrong body, the hunt for Nunu began.

Bill was summoned from Sardegna, while our doctor friend, on duty at the Clinica Gemelli, urged me to clear up the mess with the utmost expediency, as he had never heard of such a mix-up in his entire career. After an unsuccessful search of the fridge I was taken to the morgue to search round the bodies of the previous inhabitants of the intensive care unit. Eventually, we found Nunu, dressed in a pale blue nightdress, with a tag on her toe bearing the name of Mrs Moscha, looking absolutely beautiful in death.

The jigsaw was finally put together in the ward to which Nunu had been brought after her operation. There the sister told me that she had been admitted under her married name, the one in her German passport, which bore no resemblance to the name for fly! Relieved that the mystery had been cleared up, we began planning the funeral with full religious rites. Bill and I were adamant that she would have no Mozartian-style pauper's burial, however beautifully she might have sung his music.

How I regretted not looking under Nun's bed for the money, since her friends had to foot the bill, as it grew larger and larger in proportion to Nun's kidneys, which had inflated after death. Naturally, a larger coffin had to be ordered, which, to our horror, no longer complied with the measurements required for the customary burial hole in the wall. After a long search we found a temporary burial ground in a beautiful cemetery on the outskirts of the city. One of my Scottish friends, whose nerves were giving way under the strain, said, "Get her buried Quick!"

On a cold November morning, a small but loving group gathered in the hospital chapel to say farewell to Nunu. To our horror, she was laid out before us on a stretcher, dressed in black, with a hole in the toe of her stocking. Bill was so upset that he said, in his practical Ulster way, that if he had known, he would have bought her a new pair of stockings for her funeral.

While we all looked on, Nunu was coffined at the back of the church after the mass, after which the journey to her final resting place depended on how much money we had. We tipped the undertakers to put her into the hearse; to lower her into the grave, and then, just as we thought it was all over, to cover her up! Nunu, looking down from on high must have loved her funeral, taking the final curtain-call all to her wonderful self.

You may wonder why, until this point in the story, I have omitted the word "agent". Having been ripped-off on more than one occasion, I managed my own affairs until I met Ornella Cogliolo, a native of Genoa, with whom I formed an excellent collaboration and friendship which exits to this day. Ornella has a wonderful laugh and sense of humour which enables her to cope with my crazy life. In the early 1970s agents were known as "secretaries" because, under Italian law, they were illegal, which was utterly ridiculous; without their invaluable assistance artists couldn't be tracked down by opera houses and other musical establishments.

One evening, the entire musical world was stunned by the news that Italian agents, along with concert and theatre administrators from Italy's most distinguished musical institutions, had been arrested and imprisoned. It isn't everyday that one has so many friends "inside", at one time. As we all agonised for them, news spread that the Italian police were raiding their offices for files on those who had "collaborated" with this clandestine movement.

"What shall we do?", I wailed to one of my colleagues. "We'll all be in prison".

"Well", said my friend "if that happens, the entire Italian créme de la créme will be behind bars. Imagine us all making music together without having to worry about rehearsals, or catching trains and planes".

Exciting stories run the risk of becoming so embellished that they get out of hand. The original one stated that our colleagues had been handcuffed and rounded up at dawn to avoid one alerting the other of the "coup", before being bundled into a lorry and driven off in true French-revolutionary style. It made a good story until, Ornella, on her release, told me what really happened.

Early one morning, a charming young man called at her apartment to inform her that she was to accompany him to the police station. Ornella happened top be staying in an adjacent apartment while hers was being refurbished and therefore assumed that she was to be questioned about her host's activities. It was only when she asked the policeman to wait while she put on her make-up that she discovered the reason for his being there.

"You won't need make-up where you're going," he said. While Ornella dressed, he even offered to get her some newspapers to while away the time in "clink". Ornella was shown to a cell, which she shared with a noblewoman – under interrogation for her links with a terroist organisation. A special TV set was installed for her to follow the latest news on her fate, which was short-lived, because the culprits, after a slow process of elimination were all released the following night. Ornella was actually released at midnight, after her warder simply announced; "You can go now", while her aristocratic "mate" remained. Many stories reverberated round the musical grapevine which we found questionable about the conditions under which the musical hierarchy were detained; but the one about one distinguished agent nursing her favourite pillow, and finding comfort on the odd glass of her favourite wine, was true. Once released, the Italian agents immediately returned to their offices, where they carried on as if nothing had happened. Not long after, they were made legal.

Gradually engagements were pulling me northwards, away from the intimacy and protection of Rome to the Italian lakes, the Swiss border and the rest of Europe.

Every September, after a hot Italian summer, I set off to fresh mountain air and the Autunno Musicale Festival, centred around the magnificent Lake Como, close to the Swiss border. Concerts are held in some of the beautiful churches in the area or at the festival's headquarters, the beautiful Villa Olmo, overlooking the lake.

I sang both modern and classical repertoire for this happy

band of people, with whom I formed a close rapport. Through their influence, I was appointed singing professor at the distinguished Accademia Bossi in Como where, during my time there, I learnt more from teaching others about the art of singing than in my entire career. I was heartbroken when the Accademia was amalgamated and given the status of a conservatoire. Because I was not an Italian national, I was no longer eligible to teach there. Someone suggested that I should go to an old people's home and marry an ailing Italian, but I wasn't that desperate!

My connection with Como soon spread over the border to Lugano, where I became quite a regular at the Swiss Italian radio. There I was able to retreat into my oratorio roots, singing wonderful music by Handel and Bach. On one visit I vividly remember having to go to a Swiss dentist to have a filling replaced; it cost as much as I was being paid for the transmission. But when the audience complimented me on my beautiful singing, and not on my vocal aerobics, it was worth it all.

During rehearsals in Lugano for a Handel oratorio, the conductor, equipped with a stopwatch, kept changing his mind about the speeds of my arias, which naturally had to be fitted into recording time. I said nothing; I didn't need to; my transparent face did it all for me! After the rehearsal, while our bass colleague drove us to downtown Lugano in his Beetle, you can imagine my embarrassment when the conductor turned round to me in the back seat and said: "Madame Wright, you think I'm a terrible conductor, don't you?" Our driver, equally shocked by this unexpected outburst, nearly swerved off the road, while I struggled to regain composure and control over my facial expression. I said gently, "Oh no, Maestro, I think you're wonderful; I was just frustrated with Handel's speeds." Some years later, I bumped into the same conductor at a concert in Milan. "Ah, Madame Wright from Belfast!" he said. "A woman of great integrity." Only then did I realise he had a sense of humour and had been "having me on" all along.

I was leading such a busy life in Italy, that finding time to visit my parents for a considerable length of time was almost impossible; when I did, I dreaded the telephone call which might cut short my visit. One particular summons to my Irish home from the

Venice Biennale was action packed from the moment I got my countries mixed up.

The Italian translation for Stuttgart is Stoccarda, which I mistook for Stockholm. It was only after enquiries about exorbitant airfares from Belfast to Stockholm that the penny dropped. In the meantime, a colleague living there, whom I had immediately alerted about my impending visit, spent a feverish time running round the Swedish capital in an attempt to discover where, and what, I was going to perform. You can imagine my embarrassment when I told her that the rehearsals were in Stuttgart, while the concert was at La Fenice, Venice.

A few days before I was due to leave Ireland, I noticed that my British passport had expired, leaving little time for renewal in the UK. Because I was allowed to have two passports, I caught a boat across Carlingford Lough to the village of Omeath, in the Irish Republic. There, armed with my birth certificate, and those of my parents, I ensured that formalities for an Irish passport were completed at alarming speed.

The rehearsals went so well at the radio in Stuttgart that the great Venetian conductor and composer Bruno Maderna suggested that I should leave earlier than scheduled for Venice, so as to rest before the great event. Bruno was one of the most revered musicians of his time. Born in Venice, he was a small man, with dark hair, brown eyes, and a figure which revealed his love of good food and wine. The first time I saw him was in the 1960s, when he was principal conductor of the BBC Symphony Orchestra. I cannot say that I actually met Bruno at that point, since I was only an extra in the BBC chorus; but even then, those present were impressed by his modesty and amiable disposition. A first class composer, as well as a brilliant conductor, Bruno Maderna was a founder of the group of avant-garde composers, who met annually at Bruno's home in Darmstadt, Germany.

It so happened that my journey by train to Italy, via Switzerland, coincided with the killing of a policeman in Milan, for which the Baader-Meinhoff organisation, whose headquarters were known to be in Stuttgart, were suspected. You can imagine the reception I got at the Swiss border when, at the height of the Ulster troubles, I presented my Irish passport, revealing Belfast as my place of birth, to passport control. There and then I was ordered off the train and back to Stuttgart. I refused to budge, explaining that they must have mistaken me for an Icelandic citizen who needed a visa. In Italian only an 'S' and 'R' distinguish the two countries. I was so angry that I attracted the attention of Italian workers who were returning to the mother country on holiday. Standing behind the customs officers, they signalled to me to stand firm. Mercifully, while I screamed "I'm Irish, not Icelandic", the train pulled out of the station on its way to the Italian border. I had to promise that I would leave the train in Zurich to get an unnecessary visa from the Irish Embassy there; but I stayed on the train when I discovered that the Irish Embassy is in Berne, not Zurich.

There was more drama to come. When we reached Lugano I was ordered by Italian customs control to open my suitcase. News of the row at the German/Swiss border must have reached them, since I was the only person in the compartment to be searched. When the customs officials discovered a stick to relieve rheumatism in my suitcase, they became suspicious. Their facial expressions changed when I explained that it was medication for my aches and pains which I had bought in Ireland.

Realising that Italians are passionately interested in medical remedies, I offered it to them. Finally, convinced that I was drug-free, the customs officers left, delighted with my "gift", and the train was allowed to continue into Italy and the welcoming sight of Milan Central Station. Even more hassle was waiting for me in Venice.

At that time I needed a work permit because Ireland was not in the European Community. On arrival in Venice, I discovered that the theatre hadn't applied for one, and the chances of getting one before the concert were minimal. After the journey from hell, I simply couldn't cope with the irritating bureaucracy of the Italian police, so I decided to put my "damsel in distress act" to the test, descending to the floor in a faint worthy of any performance at La Fenice. It did the trick, and I got my work permit without further ado.

That week in Venice was also a case of the "show must go on". My father's life was drawing to a close, and typical of my parents' unselfishness, so that no one would be let down, it was decided to break off all contact with home until after the concert. He lived on for another month. It was also the last time I saw Bruno Maderna, who died so prematurely, depriving the musical world of his love, integrity and genius. Later in the book I shall tell you how his own compositions influenced my career.

During that Venetian sojourn, the Berlin Philharmonic, under the baton of Herbert von Karajan, visited La Fenice. Naturally, the concert was sold out; but to satisfy public demand, it was relayed to the square surrounding La Fenice. I had a grandstand position from my nearby bedroom window, where, free of charge, I listened to this incredible orchestra's interpretation of Beethoven's *Pastorale* symphony, with my old pal and compatriot James Galway playing the flute solos. In the stillness of a balmy September night, I shall never forget the magnificent sound he produced wafting round the superb setting.

Before my departure for Rome, I decided to take a last leisurely walk around lovely Venice. I didn't get far: striding towards me, as I approached St. Mark's Square, was the festival organiser frantically waving a telegram.

"You're staying. Dorothy is ill again."

"When is the concert?"

"The night after tomorrow."

The work in question, *Chant d'Automme* by the Russian composer Edison Denisov, was unknown to me. The music was fantastic and just right for my voice, but the French prose was another matter. Without doubt, it is not my best tongue, with the pronunciation leaving much to be desired. To make matters worse, I was about to perform before an intellectual public, who would be all too aware of my schoolroom French rendition. Fortunately for me, but not for him, my conductor friend, Marcello Panni, was in a room in the hotel directly below mine. Not only is he a fluent French speaker, having studied in Paris, but his wife is also French. Guilt still haunts me when I think of what I put that poor man through. I incessantly pestered him with telephone calls on the matter of pronunciation. Then, when I myself felt ominous signs of a sore throat and ensuing cold, Marcello had to listen to me whistling Denisov in the room to save my voice.

As the cold ominously settled on my chest, raucous signs of coughing and spluttering were added to the extraordinary noises exuding from my room, so that Marcello had to flee from the hotel because he couldn't concentrate on his orchestral scores above the din.

News of my indisposition spread quickly, while the conductor, the Spaniard Jesus Lopos-Cobos, had to face the possibility of yet another Denisov casualty. A less competent conductor could have been very nasty; he would have had every reason to be. But Maestro Lopos-Cobos turned out to be a gentleman with saint-like patience. He waited while I was dispatched to the local hospital where a wizard of a throat specialist began the task of restoring my voice in time to sing that evening. Tubes were placed up my nose and down my throat before inhalations of aerosol were administered. Then, equipped with more medicine, I was sent back to the hotel, returning to the hospital an hour before the concert was due to start. After further treatment, I set off for La Fenice with strict instructions not to use my voice, except in humming form, until a quarter of an hour before I was due to sing. In the meantime, the Biennale waited with bated breath for the latest developments – they were generously footing the bill – while the conductor should have been nominated for a Nobel Prize for patience. Afterwards, he told me that he was mighty relieved to hear my voice emerging from my dressing room, once the specialist's magic box of tricks had taken effect. The ensuing noise was not the real me, but it worked.

I was so drugged that I was on a high. Afterwards, I was informed that I gave the work a more robust rendition than the composer intended. Considering that the conductor had never heard me sing until the live performance, it was amazing that we pulled it off at all. Up until then we did have one or two "whistling" rehearsals, which meant that we had an idea of how it would go if, and when, I had a voice. As my career progressed, this form of rehearsing was to save my professional neck on many occasions.

When the reviews of the concert appeared Andrew Porter of the *Financial Times,* said that my performance of the Denisov was one of the most exciting events of the festival. At least someone had noticed my highly charged interpretation!

A month later, I was to repeat the Denisov songs, which I had grown to love, in another make-or-break crisis.

During a further visit to Rome, Dorothy Dorow, whose bad luck was gradually filling my coffers, was very excited about the wonderful new work being specially written for her – to be premiered at the Austrian Contemporary Festival in Graz – by the illustrious Italian composer Luigi Dallapiccola. One evening, a few weeks after my Venetian marathon, she called me from Switzerland. From the sound of her voice, I immediately knew that she hadn't rung up for a chat.

"Marge, I'm still ill. Can you take over the new work for me?"

"When is it?"

"Sunday night, in Austria."

I calculated that I had four days to learn the piece and get it into my voice before performing it in front of representatives of radio stations and world press. Italian publishers act with pigeon-like precision in delivering urgent scores to their performers, so I hadn't long to wait until the score of *Commiato* was propped up on my piano. I had already sung some of Dallapiccola's beautiful music and was therefore not daunted by the challenge, until confronted by his latest work. Because it had been written for someone with a higher and lighter voice, it presented major vocal difficulties for me.

In desperation, I called Maestro Dallapiccola's number in the hope that he would change some notes, but he had already left his Florence home for Austria. I often wondered how my indisposed colleague managed to persuade the Maestro to allow an unknown singer to sing such an important piece. He certainly must have had great faith in her judgement. But time was precious; and so, since there with no other option, I took an aspirin, brewed a strong pot of tea, and got down to work.

Without perfect pitch the task would have been impossible for me. Because time was precious, the alternating rhythmical changes and powerful top Cs scared the life out of me, while the thought of making a fool of myself before the BBC, who had already failed me eight times at solo auditions, and the world's musical cognoscenti didn't bear thinking about.

On the Friday morning before my encounter with destiny, I left Rome for Vienna, carefully extracting my music from my luggage in case it got lost between airports. There I was met by Peter Keuschnig, the dynamic conductor of the Kontrapunckte Ensemble, who were to accompany me in this formidable challenge. Fortunately, he spoke perfect English and immediately took me to our first rehearsal, made up of expert Viennese musicians, selected from the Vienna Philharmonic, Symphony and Radio orchestras. Vibrations, exuding brilliance, professionalism and world classicism overpowered me as I presented myself, an unprepared soloist, before this superb team, unused to working with an artist still struggling with notes and pitch. But having been forewarned, they treated me from day one with respect and patience. Once again, the whistling procedure took over, as we worked our way through the score until we all knew where we were going. On that trip, I learnt so much about "musical map reading" before attempting to sing it, that I continually use it in my own teaching and singing careers today.

After more whistling rehearsals, we set off by coach, early on the Sunday morning, for the Austrian ski resort of Mohrau, where the concert was to take place. I just soaked up the lush countryside, rich in autumn colours, in contrast to the rather sunburnt Italian landscape to which I had grown accustomed.

A feeling of utter loneliness overwhelmed me. My solo encounter with the most important concert in my life was looming before me and I hadn't even sung the work! Staying in an hotel, unable to sing a note, was hardly the ideal solution to "getting it into the voice", while I dare not have let rip on the bus. Suddenly, I looked round to find the conductor, music in hand, sitting beside me. Apparently the entire group had noticed my forlorn expression, and from then on made a combined effort to guide me through the work, yet again.

Eventually we reached Mohrau, where Maestro Dallapiccola, his wife and an entourage of luminaries were not only waiting for us but ready to assess my top notes. Suddenly, the tension and suppressed emotion within me rose to the surface: "If I had had the music a month ago," I cried, "it might have been possible to sing all the top notes in rehearsal; but if I happen to force them now, then I can't guarantee they'll be there tonight."

Those within earshot were horrified at such an outburst before a man of such distinction. But, as is so often the case, such people turn out to be the nicest of human beings. The maestro completely understood, because he, too, must have had qualms at the thought of entrusting his masterpiece to an unknown singer, whose voice he had still to hear. When I complained that I had no hotel, he ordered that one be found for me. None had been booked because I was scheduled to leave the resort for the town of Graz immediately after I had sung. The next day I was to be flown from there to Yugoslavia to rehearse with the Radio Orchestra of Ljubljana.

But the age of chivalry was not yet over. Two English journalists nobly vacated their room in a lovely inn to accommodate me. There I tried, in vain, to rest before dressing for the concert. I find those countdown hours endless. It is impossible to free one's mind from the music to be performed, or to become too relaxed, in case the adrenaline flow subsides.

At last, the dreaded hour arrived. While the festival organiser announced the replacement of the original soloist in every available language at his disposal, I felt like a lamb about to be offered up in musical sacrifice. The audience certainly gave the conductor and me a warm reception as we made our way onto the stage, where I placed the most difficult piece of music I had personally encountered on the stand below the microphone.

Then a miracle happened: just as we were about to begin my unaccompanied top note, the music stand collapsed before my eyes. While Peter and I struggled to put it back up again, the audience roared with laughter, my throat relaxed, and before I had time to place further obstacles in my path, sheer adrenaline took over, and we were off! It was all over in a flash. Peter's "know what you are doing" strategy had worked, proving that it is better to have a few consolidated rehearsals than many fruitless ones. Afterwards, Maestro Dallapiccola, with tears in his eyes, said, "The next time you sing *Commiato,* please give the final note its full value."

It just happened to be a top G, which one had to hold for a considerable length of time. It was made more difficult for me because of my brief acquaintance with the piece. Shortly after my return to Rome, I received a treasured postcard from the maestro, written in his immaculate handwriting, with a revised and shorter version of the note.

That memorable evening in the snow, recorded by the BBC and other radio stations, changed my entire life. As doors opened, others closed. Unfortunately, it was not only to be my debut, but my swan song with the musical department of the BBC, because they reverted to their old ways, after the recording was transmitted.

Maestro Dallapiccola was tickled pink when I told him that my critical mother complained that she couldn't hear my words in certain parts of the piece. In that particular section, the text was substituted with "ahs".

There was more excitement to come before the Denisov piece was performed two nights after the *Commiato* marathon. Later that night I checked into my Graz hotel, ready to fly to Ljubljana, capital of Slovenia, the following morning to rehearse with the radio orchestra. The organisers thought that it was cheaper to fly me there than to accommodate an entire orchestra in a hotel for two nights. My visit coincided with British Week in Graz, of which I was unaware until I was woken up by the Gordon Highlanders warming up their bagpipes. What I hadn't noticed in my exhausted state the previous evening was the smell of paint, to which I am allergic, in my newly decorated room. When my breakfast arrived outside my door, I opened my mouth to respond to the waiter's knock only to find that I had no voice! The paint had gone down onto my tired vocal chords during the night, which meant that for the second time running, I had no voice to sing the Denisov! I was beginning to believe it was jinxed.

When my effervescent escort arrived to take me to Graz airport, his smile soon vanished when I croaked a greeting.

"What are you going to do?" he asked.

"Go on to Yugoslavia. It isn't a cold, and I have two days to get my voice back," I said as nonchalantly as I could manage.

On arrival at the small airport, I expected to find a queue of passengers waiting to board a flight; but, apart from a tiny two-seater parked on the tarmac before us, the place seemed to be deserted. My worst thoughts were confirmed when a dashing young man swooped down on me with an invitation to follow him to a section where travel formalities were completed. Then, with great charm and chivalry, he escorted me to the two-seater plane which I had spotted from the safety of the airport lounge. It's not often I am panic-stricken, but I was then.

"We're not going in that!" I yelled. But my protests were in vain, since I had no other option but to climb into the plane, as if I were getting into a car. I'd have swopped it for one there and then. Luggage wasn't a problem; there wasn't any because, after the rehearsal, I was to return to Graz that evening. I consoled myself with the thought that if I were going to meet my maker, it would be in the company of a handsome young pilot, whose excellent command of English could warn me of impending disaster.

Mercifully, the weather was ideal for flying. We travelled over an expanse of breathtaking mountain scenery, bathed in glorious sunshine. I was so quiet that the pilot became worried.

"Are you without a voice from fear, or from a cold?" he asked.

Above the din of the engines, I croaked that I was actually enjoying the flight. Then, to relieve the silence, I asked him if he flew that route regularly.

"Oh no," he replied. "I'm a law student. I belong to the Graz Flying Club. Flying is just my hobby." For the first time in my life, I was speechless!

When arriving at airports, artists are usually left to their own devices, unless they are a superstar. But in Ljubljana, I was surprised to see a smart, chauffeur-driven Mercedes on hand to pick us up, as, at that time, the former Yugoslavia was an Eastern Bloc country.

A hotel, with lunch included, had been specially reserved for our visit, and I took full advantage of it. But the main priority was the restoration of my voice. It was then that I remembered a colleague telling me of a similar plight when, with the help of a bottle of red wine, and in the privacy of his own dressing room, he literally gargled his way through a three-act opera in Rome. And so, after a dose of the same "medicine", which I had swiped from the lunch table, I administered a dose, with amazing results. By the time the car came to collect me, not only was I miraculously steady on my feet, but I had a voice and cheeks that glowed with health.

After the rehearsal, which went remarkably well under the circumstances, I mentioned to the conductor, Samuel Hubad, that I was returning to Graz on a private plane. "Rather you than me" were his comforting words. On the other hand, the solo cellist, Heinrich Schiff, offered to take my place. He obviously liked private planes more than I did.

Once again, the Mercedes was waiting to take me to the airport. We nearly forgot the pilot, until we saw him frantically waving to us outside the hotel where we had left him. His main worry was that we might have to return there for the night, owing to strict rules about private aircraft flying in Yugoslavian airspace after dark. But we just made it, and in no time at all were once again installed in our mini plane. A great deal of frantic searching went on while the pilot, unused to flying in that particular model, searched for the lights. At last he found them, and we were waved away by a man holding two yellow bats, and the passengers in a DC9 towering above us.

Weather conditions were not as favourable as on the outward journey, with a strong wind blowing against us. To complicate matters, communication with the control tower, conducted in English, was very faint and crackly. Eventually, contact with Graz airport was resumed, and we prepared to land. On the approach, the pilot casually informed me that we would have to circle because the landing lights hadn't been switched on. Once they knew we were coming, we landed safely, much to my relief.

My handsome companion offered me a lift from the airport into town in his Alfa Romeo, an experience which was even more hair-raising than being airborne.

Back in the hotel, I was so shaken by the day's adventures that I made straight to the bar, where a group of English policemen, in Graz for British Week, took one look at my ashen face and bought, me a double brandy.

In the meantime, the paint in my room had dried out, and I was as right as rain; so much so, that I actually looked forward to the concert. Being on more familiar terms with the Denisov songs certainly eased my troubled mind. This was also obvious to those who had heard the Venetian rendition; a representative of the Canadian Broadcasting Corporation asked me which version was the authentic one – the hysterical or more tranquil interpretation.

The following morning I set off from Graz airport as a normal passenger, travelling back to Vienna on a scheduled Austrian Airways flight. Since I was in no rush to return home to Rome, I decided to unwind and treat myself by checking back into the lovely hotel, which I hadn't had time to enjoy, and from which I had set put on my exciting adventures of the intervening days.

Vienna was sheer bliss, and that evening I went to the State Opera to see Franco Zefferelli's production of *Don Giovanni*. It was a wonderful climax to my visit, which heralded a new phase in my career, as well as the beginning of a musical love affair with Vienna.

Chapter 5

Bouncing Along

When I was invited to sing at Palermo's prestigious Teatro Massimo I was thrown into the operatic world right at the deep end, panic-stricken and totally without experience.

I had already performed in Sicily in 1970 when I gave a recital in Messina with Robert Kettleson, the American pianist who went on to become an indispensable repeteteur at La Scala, Milan and later, at Paris's Bastille opera house. One of the highlights of our trip was when our train from Rome was manoeuvred onto a ship, which ferried us from the Italian mainland, across the Strait of Messina, to Sicily.

Before we rehearsed the following morning, we went into a newsagent's in Messina to buy a newspaper. At that time, there was such a shortage of Italian currency that one was liable to receive anything from aspirin and sweets to suppositories, in lieu of currency. After this happened to us, we later returned to the shops to buy something with our "change". At first the assistant refused, but once Bob and I had argued our case the suppositories were accepted as legal tender.

I had previously passed through Palermo on my way to holiday on the island of Lampedusa. Even then, after a long train journey from Milan to Trapani – where my friend and I caught the ferry to the island, I got the impression that this capital city of Sicily was both noisy and chaotic. Motorbikes, cars, you name it, whizz by at an alarming speed, while passing riders on Vespas can, in a flash, dexterously whip your handbag, or other valuables, from you.

Nevertheless, the Sicilian sunshine has such a calming effect on one's nervous system, that it feels wonderful to be alive in such a climate. Unfortunately, no magic potion could have calmed my troubled soul as I "clocked in" at the stage door of the Massimo for the first rehearsal.

The enormity of the building was enough to intimidate any novice. Considered to one of the world's largest opera houses, it was both monumental and forbidding, to say the least, with imposing Corinthian columns adorning its facade. Those of you familiar with *The Godfather* films will be interested to know that the bloody scenes leading up to the "death" of Don Corleone, played by Al Pacino, were shot on the front steps of this famous theatre.

Having shunned the opera class at college in favour of a more academic course, I had no idea of how to make an exit or entrance, let alone co-ordinate music and movement. My only previous stage experience stemmed from school and amateur dramatics. The task might have been less daunting if it hadn't been the Massimo, where so many famous singers had sung. Owing to its refurbishment, we were transferred for the performances to Palermo's other impressive and famous Politeama theatre.

The opera to be performed was *Il Prigioniero,* by Luigi Dallapiccola, on whose recommendation I was invited to sing the part of the desolate mother, distraught over the impending death of her son. Because of my lack of operatic experience, I was more than apprehensive as I set off to the first rehearsal with piano, and to meet the French conductor Antonio de Almeida. All went well until production rehearsals, which were a complete nightmare. Not only was I all thumbs and feet but psychologically paralysed in front of the entire company, who were old hands at the game.

Realising that I was becoming a burden to all concerned, I decided to get to grips with the situation or resign. And so, I spent an entire afternoon before my bedroom mirror, desperately working out a way round my inhibited movements. By the time evening rehearsal arrived, I was ready to burst into the room with all the confidence of a prima donna.

"I going to give my interpretation of this role," I proclaimed. "If you don't like it, then trim it up".

I didn't care if I made a fool of myself, which I'm sure I did, while our lovely producer – tongue in cheek – judged it to be a performance worthy of Maria Callas herself – the great Greek opera singer – after which we all settled down to work like one big happy family.

Palermo was glorious in the Sicilian spring sunshine, enabling us to spend time by the sea, where panoramic restaurants specialised in seafood. It certainly was a wonderful way to live, singing superb music in an idyllic atmosphere of lovely people, wine, sunshine and song, for which we were actually being paid. Many balmy evenings were spent eating in a pizzeria, from which we could gaze up at the magnificently floodlit cathedral of Monreale, one of Sicily's many picturesque sights.

Built along the bay, at the foot of Monte Pellegrino, Palermo is full of history and culture. During Arab domination its beauty was compared to that of Cairo; sadly, the massive bombardments of 1943 destroyed most of it. But the Middle Eastern influence can still be found in its historic churches.

Palermo was also the home of Giuseppe Tommasi, Prince of Lampedusa, who wrote the novel *The Leopard*, which was made into the famous film, starring Burt Lancester and Claudia Cardinale. By sheer coincidence, his real-life adopted son, Giacchino Lanza Tommasi, was the artistic director of Teatro Massimo, and the lovely man responsible for my operatic debut in *Il Prigionero*. You shall hear more about him later. Unfortunately, glamorous as it may seem, singers are like airline crews, who are so busy working that they have little time to appreciate the interesting places they visit.

The pressures imposed on those contracted to Italian opera houses are immense. A foreign artist is expected to be endowed with the artistic skill and technique which the Italians have in abundance. One works as part of a team, without histrionics, until sheer perfection is reached, producing a pattern of sleep, work, eating, work and sleep, until opening night and beyond.

At the preview a charming man, who had heard me sing at the dress rehearsal, came round to my dressing room, exuding praise and assuring me of thunderous applause from him and his "friends". I was flattered until my tenor colleague enlightened me. My admirer was the head of the claque, a band of opera buffs who cheer, or boo, the singers according to how much money you pay their leader. On one occasion I myself was brought along in such a role to the Rome Opera where, without having to pay, I applauded under instructions, unaware of the implications involved.

Nevertheless, the first night was a gala event, full of excitement as flowers and telegrams arrived to add cheer and atmosphere to our dressing rooms. As for the elegance of the audience, we were in Italy, the home of class and fashion. At a gala opening, gowns by Valentino or Versace are shown off by ladies who are more interested in glamour and money, than the opera on stage. But it is the mink coat which dominates haute couture in Italy, what ever the weather may be like. If you don't have one, then you are not *alla mode*.

After the first night, the real opera lovers began to fill the theatre. The remaining performances took place every other day and jogged along perfectly until some of the scene-shifters, bored with the routine, decided to take a nap. The mother's aria actually opens the opera, lamenting the plight of her son, before ending on a top B flat which, in that particular production, is sustained at full power during a walk backwards, and off stage, through a set of screens which have to be opened at a precise moment to allow her to pass.

I lived in constant fear of backing into one of them if this didn't happen. My worst fears came true when, at the third performance, I heard loud snores coming from behind the screens, just as I was holding on like grim death to my top note. Suddenly, the situation was saved when I heard someone say: "Wake up, wake up, she's on her way!" Mercifully, my path was cleared just in time to avoid a nasty collision.

Before I signed the Palermo contract, I had to fulfil another to sing at a concert for the Filarmonica of Rome with my old pals, the Kontrapunckte Ensemble from Vienna, whom I hadn't met since our hair-raising encounter in Graz. The only problem was that it meant making a quick dash from Palermo to Rome and back, in between performances. Since the artistic director of Teatro Massimo, Giacchino Lanza Tommasi, also held the corresponding appointment with the Filarmonica, I was given permission to fulfil both contracts. Giacchino has always been a good friend to me throughout my career. Aware of the fact that I was an operatic novice, he signed me up for seven performances at the third largest opera house in the world, later explaining that my "feathered" performance in Venice, at which he was present, was sufficient proof that I could act.

Coming from a family which is quite paranoid about arriving on time, the idea of "sandwiching" jobs together has always scared me stiff. I was in a state of turmoil for days before I was due to fly to Rome after a performance in Palermo, then perform there before returning to Palermo in time to sing at an evening performance the next day. Naturally, because I had no understudy, the conductor was worried that I might not make in back in time. Moreover, to complicate matters, the travel agent informed me that the Sirocco, was forecast. This ominously meant that planes might be diverted from Palermo to Catania, endangering my little jaunt.

The Sirocco is a wind coming from Africa; it causes one to perspire profusely, as witnessed by those who saw the film *Death In Venice*, when the sweat and hair-dye ran down Dirk Bogarde's face while he lay dying in a deck chair on the beach.

On the outward journey from the airport we were able to depart on time, which was reassuring because of Palermo's exposure to cross-winds and unnerving proximity to the sea. It was great to be back in Rome for a day. Weeks spent away from home on one's own can be very lonely indeed, especially for someone like me who, at that time, liked to let my hair down in between demanding singing assignments.

The concert with my Viennese friends was a great success and led to even more wonderful meetings with Rainer Keuschnig, the ensemble's superb pianist.

Switching styles was not one of my strong points at that time, creating difficulties for me in coming to terms with *Schliesse Mir Die Augen Beide*, by Alban Berg. It certainly contrasted with the more robust tones I had been using in the opera in Palermo. Rainer nearly had a fit when he heard my full-blooded rendition of the more refined Berg, so I decided to hand him the reins, since the song was from his Viennese background and language.

It went so well that an encore would have been in order, but we decided to just acknowledge the bows and not chance our luck a second time round. How was I to know that it was only the beginning of "listening to what Rainer said" as our brief appearance inspired us to form a lieder duo, about more of which later. After the concert we all went to a wonderful pizzeria, The Capriccioso, which was to become our "local" for future meetings in Rome. We finally parted company around 2 am, when the lads went to bed, while I, instead of returning to my own apartment, headed out to the airport where I "cat-napped" until it was time to leave on the first plane out to Palermo at 5 am.

I heaved a sigh of relief when we took off on time since ours was the only plane to land at Palermo that day. After a call to the conductor's hotel to reassure him that he would have a singer for the afternoon's performance, I slept the day away until it was time to go to the theatre. There I was met by a distraught colleague with the alarming news that my agent had arrived and reported both the claque and the "friendly" man to the administration of Teatro Massimo.

"If you don't put things right now, you will be booed off the stage," he warned me. It transpired that, in my absence, my agent had informed the artistic director that I had practically been threatened-at-gun-point to pay up – or else. I was livid at such distortion of an innocent, passing remark. I had merely told her that in future I would add on to my fee what amounted to protection money. There and then the head of the mob was brought to my dressing room where, before Giacchino, I exonerated him from all blame. A few hours later the applause which I personally received was more thunderous than the opening night. The poor man could have lost his job, all because of an agent's slanderous allegations. After that episode I sacked *her*.

The 1970s brought about the Dallapiccola era, a period in which I was not only invited to sing the works of this great man, but to study them under his personal guidance. With hindsight, I was so lucky to live in the same country as this guru, and within travelling distance of his home in Florence.

It could have come out of the film *A Room With A View*, I stayed in the Pensione Annalena, in the same palazzo as the maestro's apartment, and spent hours wandering round the beautiful churches and seeing the art treasures for which Florence is so famous. I used to treat myself to a meal at the Trattoria La Sostanza, frequented by the great painter Annigoni, where I enjoyed a substantial Florentine steak, accompanied by a healthy salad, before tucking into a special meringue sweet topped with thick cream. In those days I could afford to indulge in such extravagance because, after burning off calories in strenuous rehearsals, I was as thin as a rake. It was there that I ate when I went to Florence to rehearse for a concert to be held in Perugia, under the patronage of Signora Alba Buitoni, of the famous pasta dynasty. The programme, accompanied by the orchestra of Florence's Maggio Musicale, was in honour of Dallapiccola's seventieth birthday. The three soloists were a lovely young Italian mezzo-soprano, the great Hungarian-born soprano Magda Laszlo, a renowned interpreter of Dallapiccola's music, who performed the major part of the concert, while I ended the evening with *Commiato*.

Years earlier, I had heard Madga sing the role of Poppea in a production at Glyndebourne of Monteverdi's *Incoronazione Di Poppea*, in which she not only sang divinely, but looked gorgeous. When we eventually met in the Anglo-American Hotel in Florence, I found her as charming in private life as she was on stage, with a wonderful sense of humour and anecdotes to share over meals. It was wonderful to be with a great singer without the customary egotistical airs of a prima donna. She was also a tower of strength through some very trying rehearsals in Florence, when I had difficulty in adjusting to a different approach to the work from that of the Viennese group at the premiere.

In due course, I was to discover that each conductor has a different approach to the timing and phrasing of *Commiato*, turning my work into a complicated nightmare. In a one-to-one situation, everything would have been fine, but an enthusiastic vocal coach, whose job was to make sure that I was familiar with the music, nearly drove me mad. He continually interrupted the proceedings to correct irrelevant details, of which I was well aware, having already studied and performed the work. As rehearsals laboured on, my anguish, coupled with the pain in my throat, grew worse.

It was relieved only by sips of grappa mixed with camomile tea, recommended by Magda, who had herself been in similar situations throughout her career.

When Maestro Dallapiccola arrived to supervise the final rehearsal, he found me sitting in isolation waiting to be summoned into the rehearsal room. When he enquired how the rehearsals were going, I confessed that I was finding the task of imitating sopranos of great fame not only daunting, but impossible. The maestro took a deep breath before giving his version of his masterpiece.

"I am a composer who knows what he is writing about," he said. "If I had wanted the soloist to imitate others, I'd have written it into the score."

There and then we made an appointment to meet at his house the following morning, and it was there I learnt more about the art of singing than from any teacher. The maestro disliked tape recorders, yet consented to record the text in an identical speech modulation to its musical counterpart. He also explained that he always set the music to the words, and not the other way round. A little bit of history was made that day because my amateur tape recording is one of the few of him in conversation. On that memorable morning, the maestro confessed to me that, because of his perfectionism and keen sense of pitch, people were generally in awe of him. He took me by surprise when he said, "Are you, Marjorie?"

"Yes," I said, "that is why I'm here!"

I never sang *Commiato* from that meeting until the concert; instead, I spoke the text in time to the tape, which made a welcome change from whistling.

My elegantly dressed colleagues were a hard act to follow. The Dallapiccolas described the event as a *fila di Moda* – a fashion show – expressing delight that we all "weren't dressed up like Christmas trees".

After undeserved encouragement from Magda, I took a few deep breaths before I went out and gave my all, at the end of which, and to rapturous applause, the conductor Zoltán Peskó and I warmly embraced. It was the first of many wonderful concerts with him. Hungarian-born, and a former assistant to the

American conductor Lorin Maazel at the Deutsche Opera in Berlin, Zóltan is not only a fine conductor and musician but great fun too.

Perugia, through Amici Della Musica, the concert society run by Signora Buitoni, was my lucky venue. Owing to her interest in my career, I performed with many celebrated people, among whom were Bruno Canino, the brilliant pianist, who went on to form a duo with the violinist Itzhak Perlman, and the American piano duo, Gold and Fitzdale. I supplied a quartet of singers to perform Brahms *Libesliederwaltzer* with them at a Perugian concert. There was some concern at the Sunday morning rehearsal when the contralto discovered that she had left her evening shoes at home in Rome. By a stroke of luck, she tracked down the proprietor of a shoe shop, who, before legal Sunday trading was introduced, opened up specially for her.

A great treat was when artists were invited to dine at the beautiful Buitoni villa, where Signora Alba would bring us up-to-date with musical news. On that special evening when Dallapiccola was honoured, the maestro himself was in splendid form. He had a wonderful habit of taking a cigarette from his pocket before saying "Senta" ("listen" in Italian). Then, while we waited with bated breath, he would put the cigarette into its holder before continuing with the story, which was never without a witty turn of phrase.

It wasn't long before Zoltán Peskó and I met again. This time the venue was Naples, where *Commiato* was to be performed at a concert organised by the Italian radio at their studios there.

Originally Dorothy Dorow had been engaged to perform the work; but once again, continuing health problems had prevented her travelling to Naples, resulting in yet another SOS summoning me to deputise for her at the last minute. Zóltan was worried that I wouldn't make it in time and was waiting for me in the foyer of the hotel. My arrival also happened to coincide with a football match in a huge stadium close by my hotel. Fortunately, I was able to avoid the crowds by getting there while the match was still in progress, since the Italians are both passionate about their football and the outrageous fees paid for, and to, their star players.

Naples can be hazardous. Every time I go there, I feel that I am taking my life in my hands by venturing out alone. One is reminded of the saying 'See Naples and die' when one sees monumental horse-drawn carriages, bedecked with plumes, carrying its citizens, accompanied by the sound of cars hooting their way through traffic jams, to their final resting place. Beautiful as Naples may be, I never relaxed while working there, because thieves are notoriously prevalent, pouncing out from the most unexpected places to snatch handbags and valuables, and then making off at speed on Vespas.

To return to the RAI – the Italian radio – the first rehearsal went well, enabling me to relax and actually look forward to the concert – except that it didn't take place! That evening, the conductor and I, dressed in our evening finery, set out for the concert hall in a taxi. Almost at once we were immediately brought to a halt by a huge demonstration of protesting metalworkers, surrounded by mounted police. Since strikes are an everyday occurrence in Italy, we just took it in our stride until we reached the RAI, where we discovered that our engineers, without whom the concert could not be recorded, had also joined the demonstrators. This meant that not only were our efforts fruitless, but, owing to the sudden departure of those in charge of our pay packets, the possibility of non-payment loomed. Normally we would have been handsomely paid in cash after the concert, but on this occasion we were informed that the matter would have to be thrashed out after the weekend at headquarters in Rome.

Fortunately, I had brought sufficient funds to cover expenses; when payment is not forthcoming, hotels and restaurants can make singing an expensive hobby.

Our Friday evening wasn't entirely a disaster because the Duke Franceso D'Avola, a friend and colleague of Zóltan Peskó, who had come to hear us perform, invited both of us to dinner at an exclusive restaurant overlooking the Bay of Naples. He was a close relative of the exiled Italian royal family. Over dinner he invited us both to a grand luncheon party he was hosting the following day at his villa. Zoltán didn't want to go because he, like me, wasn't too keen on cocktail parties; but, since our delightful host was so insistent, we decided to delay our journey back to Rome and accept his invitation.

It turned out to be a very splendid event indeed. It was held, in glorious sunshine, in the Duke's magnificent home overlooking the sea. His face lit up when he saw us in the line of elegantly clad guests waiting to be received by him and his noble mother. At first, we couldn't understand why we weren't being offered some of the wonderful goodies displayed on the buffet table. The reason was soon revealed when a hush fell over the gathering while our host escorted a lady into the room, before whom everyone either curtsied or bowed.

From reading Italian magazines, I instantly recognised the Duchess of Aosta, wife of the nephew of the ex-King of Italy, and daughter of the Comte de Paris. Her photographs did not do her justice; she had the bluest eyes and most gorgeous figure, combined with French panache, I have ever seen.

On my return to Rome, one of my friends, an ardent Neapolitan monarchist, was green with envy when I told her where I had been.

"How on earth did you manage an invitation to that reception?" she asked. "I couldn't get one for love or money."

Later that evening, Zóltan and I returned to Rome. Before parting at the railway station, we arranged to meet two days later at the RAI headquarters to fight for our rights. After a lot of hard bargaining, a financial compromise was reached, from which we were paid half our original fees. Zoltán sent his to the Musicians' Benevolent Fund, while I kept mine and said nothing. Apart from the fact that one cannot take on a big institution, like the RAI, single-handedly and win, I certainly needed them more than they needed me.

Once again, another visit southwards took me to Bari for a series of Holy Week concerts. They were conducted by an elderly Sicilian composer, who had set some charming poems by Salvatore Quasimido to equally lovely music which, combined with the *Four Last Songs* by Richard Strauss, which I hadn't sung since my student days, made a truly interesting programme.

Two of the concerts took place in the magnificent Teatro Petrozelli, where the acoustics were ideal for the soaring high notes of the Strauss songs and the beautiful violin solo in my favourite one, *Beim Schlafangen* with the haunting melody becoming entwined with the soprano solo.

The remaining concerts were held in villages throughout this lovely region of Puglia, which was obviously unaccustomed to visits of such magnitude. When we attempted to perform in a church, where, as the only obvious soloist, I had only to sing four songs, our concert was misinterpreted by the audience as an extension of 'mass will a full symphony orchestra', which had just been celebrated. Mothers with babes in arms walked obliviously round the church, talking at the tops of their voices, while their offspring screamed so loudly that the orchestral accompaniment was inaudible. As for my voice, it just disappeared into thin air. Suddenly, the conductor turned round in the middle of my song and shouted, "Shut up, shut up!" in Italian, after which I carried on singing in a somewhat more restrained atmosphere.

The following evening, on Holy Thursday, we were taken by coach to another hillside village and deposited outside a lovely little theatre furbished in gold and red. There a brief rehearsal was held before the audience arrived. To our utter dismay, only two people turned up. We dutifully serenaded them until sounds coming from further up the street gradually drew nearer and drowned us out. It transpired that our concert had coincided with a religious procession, headed by a brass band, which was solemnly followed by the entire population of the village whom we had hoped to entertain inside the theatre. As the two members of our audience left after the interval to join the procession, we all packed up and went back to Bari.

Our final concert took place in the Petrozelli, before a packed house. Tragically, it suffered the same fate as that other lovely opera house, La Fenice, Venice. Both were destroyed by fire. It is enough to make one weep. At the end of that wonderful evening, a charming gentleman, introducing himself as the director of the Bari Conservatoire, congratulated me on my singing of the Strauss songs. Later he joined us, the conductor, myself and the organisers of the festival, at a nearby restaurant where, with gusto, we tucked into the specialities of the house. After we had eaten everything in sight, he insisted on footing the bill for the party. When I protested that we should all "go Dutch" the conductor said, "Let him pay; he can afford it." Only then did I discover that he was Nino Rota, who composed the music for *The Godfather* films.

The opera house of San Carlo in Naples is one of the most beautiful and well known in Italy. I was contracted to go there on a ten-day assignment, which I thought rather excessive just to sing Wagner's wonderful *Wesendonck Lieder*, lasting no more than twenty minutes in performance. In the interim, hotel and restaurant expenses had to be paid out of my own pocket before being settled, in cash, at the end of the performance.

I arrived at the first rehearsal to find that the orchestra was in complete disarray because they hadn't been paid for months. Some even had to send in deputies who were in a more affluent position to pay for petrol to and from rehearsals. In such financial instability, my heart sank at the thought of having to fork out for a ten-day stay in Naples. Having signed a contract, I had no option but to stay put.

The conductor, an elderly Hungarian, and, like all his compatriots in the business, a marvellous musician, was eccentric, to say the least. He was so dissatisfied with the theatre's scores of Beethoven's *Ninth Symphony* that he went all the way back to his home in Switzerland to fetch his own markings and scores. During his absence I had to remain for three days in my hotel near the harbour, from which I didn't dare emerge after 8 pm I had blond hair then, to which Neapolitans are attracted; not just mine, but anybody's.

During my enforced holiday I became a tourist, "doing" the museums and treating myself to a day trip to Capri, which was both disappointing and too touristy for my taste. An interesting feature though was the house of Alex Munthe, author of *The Story of San Michelle*. I shall never forget my solitary fortieth birthday in Naples. If I had been working I would have been surrounded by people; instead, I spent the evening in my hotel bedroom with a pizza, and a bottle of plonk to lull me into oblivion.

I did make up for it on my return to Rome, where I spent an entire week living it up, believing that life begins at forty. Little did I know that it was to be the most traumatic and soul-searching period of my life.

Back at the opera house, the conductor's return was greeted

with orchestral mayhem, as the financial crisis had still not been resolved. The players couldn't have cared less, and I didn't blame them; among other things they had to contend with a conductor, who had little or no knowledge of Italian, and threw tantrums in English and German. When the situation got really out of hand he appealed to me to inform the orchestra that he was about to have a heart attack. Italian grammar can be complicated, especially the use of the subjunctive tense, with which I was not totally familiar. As I related my heart-rending appeal, with the conductor still on his feet, the orchestra howled with laughter as I became entangled with the grammar. The conductor, on the other hand, nearly did have a heart attack from rage, because he thought the laughter was directed at him. After I reassured him, calm was restored.

Although we rehearsed at San Carlo, the two concerts took place in the garden of the Villa Ruffulo, where Wagner wrote the third act of *Parsifal.* Located at Ravello, high up on the rocks of the Amalfi coastline, it provided the ideal setting for the performance of his lovely songs.

Just up the road was the superb Hotel Palombo, at that time owned by Swiss proprietors, whose hospitality and superb cooking made up for the heat of Naples and the week's solitude. American fellow guests took me down to the town of Ravello and the breathtaking Amalfi coastline, with the sea shimmering in the glorious morning sunshine. It was here along its hair-pin bends that *The Italian Job,* starring Michael Caine, was filmed; in fact, the roads are so narrow that only one bus is allowed to pass between Amalfi and Sorrento. Halfway between these two beauty spots is the lovely fishing village of Positano, where luxury yachts are moored. I was so invigorated by all there was to see that by the time concert hour approached, I was in a real holiday mood, rearing to go.

The concert was not without its dramatic moments. Just as we were about to begin the Wagner, the conductor noticed that the brass section was not the one with which he had rehearsed. Naturally, this caused some on-stage friction, while the audience and I looked on. Eventually, we got under way. All went well until a gentle breeze began to waft round the platform above the cliff. Loose orchestral parts were caught up out and carried out to sea. I continued with the last song of the cycle after –out of nowhere –

clothes pegs were produced to pin back retrieved scores onto music stands.

The climax of the evening was a scrumptious spread laid on by the Palombo in their magnificent torch-lit gardens, again over-looking the sea. It left a memory to savour.

The next month I was back in Sicily, after I was recalled from a break in Ireland to sing the lovely Quasimodo songs at the festival of Taormina. It is a fashionable seaside resort to which Italians flock to escape the intense August heat. The concert was to take place around the 15th, known as *ferragosto*, when towns and cities are deserted, except for tourists. The problem on that particular occasion was the availability of flights to Catania, in Sicily, as well as accommodation in overcrowded Taormina. Fortunately, my agent Ornella was in charge of arrangements at the Italian end and advised me to get a flight out of Belfast, via Heathrow, to Milan, before taking it from there. *En route*, I stopped off in London to buy an evening dress in a lovely colour of jade. Serendipity was at work, because it couldn't have been a better choice for the Graeco-Roman backdrop against which I was to sing. It cost £10 in the sales and, being drip-dry, went on to grace many hotel bathrooms.

Back in Rome, Ornella had miraculously found a cancellation on a flight to Catania on one of the hottest Sunday afternoons imaginable. We were met on arrival by a young boy holding aloft placards with my name and that of the famous Belgian violinist Arthur Grumiaux. He led the way through crowds of homecoming Sicilians and their welcoming families, to the luggage bay. It took some pushing and shoving to retrieve our luggage, before we set off for Taormina in a limousine.

Maestro Grumiaux and his elegant wife sat with me in the back of the car where, to relieve an awkward silence, I asked the great soloist what he was going to play – a rather obvious question to ask someone with a violin case on his lap.

"The violin," he patiently replied.

"What piece are you playing?" I enquired, as I plodded on further into the mire.

"Beethoven's *Violin Concerto*."

"Which one?" I persisted,

"There is only one!"

After that faux pas, we continued the rest of the journey in silence.

We were driven up to a very swanky hotel flying the flags of all nations, where long-term reservations had only been made for Arthur Grumiaux and his wife, while I was to be turned out next morning. Unprepared for a fashion-conscious ambience, I decided to eat my money's worth after an evening swim in the pool, for which I casually flung my dressing gown over my bikini and walked into the foyer without anyone even noticing. I simply didn't care, since, with a packed Taormina, camping out on the beach for the rest of my stay was not out of the question.

Next morning, I trod my weary way up to the festival office, where an official found a lovely room in an old-fashioned hotel adjacent to the temple where I was to perform. Meals were served on a long terrace menacingly overlooked by Mount Etna, the famous volcano, which I feared would erupt at any minute.

I even bumped into old friends. I received my first surprise while warming up in a hall, just off the village square, when someone knocked on my door; it was my first operatic producer from Palermo, who had come to cheer me on. When I returned to the square I heard a group of young men shouting "Marjorie" from outside bar. They were my "fans" from Milan, who had made the journey to Sicily to hear me sing.

Because of the intense heat the concert was held late at night in the spectacular ruins of the Graeco-Roman temple looking out over the sea where, with the Romanian Radio Orchestra and its conductor; one just relaxed, absorbed, and let the voice do it all.

Paris in springtime should inspire romantic visions, but alas, it didn't quite turn out that way when I went there to sing the role of the mother in a concert version of Dallapiccola's great opera, *Ulysees*, for the Paris radio. The opera was premiered in Berlin before going on to La Scala, Milan, where it was enthusiastically received. It was there that the conductor added extra markings to the huge score before the publisher, obviously unaware of the changes, forwarded them to Paris. From the moment they arrived all hell broke loose.

I had worked with the German conductor Ernest Boeur on

numerous occasions on a one-to-one basis. Then we had got along famously, possibly because neither of us spoke the other's language well enough to become personally acquainted, with exchanges limited to "enchantez", "bonjour" and "bon soir".

There were thirteen soloists in an international cast. But the large French choir and orchestra decided to voice their disapproval at the hard work in no uncertain terms. The frustrated conductor, furious at the complicated markings made to the original score, took it out on the cast, who stuck together throughout the tempestuous week in a display of solidarity. My colleagues, most of whom were Americans working in German opera houses, were the greatest fun to be with, especially my baritone colleague from the American deep south, who was on honeymoon with his delightful English bride. Everyone magnanimously defended me when I unwittingly brought a rebelliously driven week to an almighty climax.

It all came to a head when a radio engineer asked me to sing my forcefully dramatic top notes to assess the volume level required for the transmission, so I dutifully obliged by taking one almighty breath and letting them have it. Even my own head spun from the force of the blast, while my colleagues collapsed in giggles.

As I said before, French has never been one of my greatest assets, so when the conductor addressed me after my dramatic declamation, I was too embarrassed to tell him that I hadn't understood him. Still reeling from my interpretation of the mother's anguish, I opted for the easy way out, and said, "Oui". That the word "yes" in French could have had such an impact on a final rehearsal was beyond belief. The conductor, with the head of the radio on his heels, stormed out of the hall threatening not to return. While we all sat there, wondering if there would be a concert or not, my American colleague leant towards me and asked, in his rich fruity tone, if I had understood what the conductor had meant. When I confessed that I hadn't a clue, he told me that the conductor, having had such wrath hurled at him by my top notes, had enquired if I was angry with him. By saying "yes", I had put my big feet right in it. After a lunch adjournment, when the conductor was persuaded to stay, I explained, through an interpreter, that I had completely misunderstood the question, after which all was forgiven.

The concert took place in an atmosphere of musical anarchy, yet attracted favourable reviews in the French press. Nevertheless, it was sad to see state-employed musicians behaving in such an irresponsible way, just because they weren't allowed to sing what they wanted. There is an extraordinary ending to this story: nearly twenty eight years later The French radio resurrected the transmission of *Ulysses* from its archives and issued it, to critical acclaim, as a CD.

We didn't see much of Paris because, as happens during most of these trips to exciting places, we were entombed at the radio concert hall. We did, however, have one free day, May Day, which was a national holiday, when everything, including the Louvre, was closed. Instead, I wandered along the Seine, where the Oxford and Cambridge boat crews were competing. It was hard to believe that the Seine had been exchanged for the River Thames, yet a small crowd of English supporters gathered along the banks of the river to cheer them on, just the same.

The next port of call in our journey is Turin, situated in Italy's industrial north, from whence Fiat cars hail. It is also home to the famous Juventus football team.

Like Milan, a two-hour train journey away, Turin is a city geared to making money. Its musical institutions, like the famous Teatro Regio and the RAI, as well as its excellent prose theatre, are run in the same way. Therefore, when I visited any of these establishments, I had to adopt a more regimented attitude to my art, albeit at its expense.

An example of this occurred when I received a call from the Italian radio to deputise at the last minute for Shirley Verrett, the famous American soprano, at a public concert in Turin. When I heard the name Beethoven, my throat tightened at the very thought of reaching some of the top notes which he imposed on sopranos; but I needn't have worried, because this work was melodious and easy to sing.

Dorothy Dorow was to sing the higher part in Beethoven's heavenly work *Der Glorreiche Augenblick* for soloists, chorus and orchestra under the baton of the Florentine conductor Piero Bellugi, who was also a great raconteur.

It was nearly 5 pm in Rome when I received the summons to Turin for a 10 am call the following morning. Not only had I no ticket, but the banks were closed, leaving me without funds. Cashpoints had not yet been introduced, and, having no Visa or Mastercard, I had no access to money outside banking hours. Within an hour, a special messenger delivered a plane ticket to my door, while cash to last me during my stay was brought to Turin airport to meet me on arrival at 8 am the following morning. I used to wonder just how much money the radio was saving by hiring me instead of the indisposed American star, who would have stayed at the most exclusive hotel, while I, "the local", had to do with less.

It wasn't long before I was back in Turin, when another American soprano had to pull out of a concert performance of Hindemith's opera *Sancta Susanna*. The opera has only two pro-tagonists; a soprano, who portrays a nun about to be buried alive in a wall, and the more imposing contralto in the role of Mother Superior.

From day one I was completely overwhelmed by my contralto colleague, also an American, who resembled a Jackie Onassis look-a-like. While I stayed in a dingy two-star hotel, she was in a five-star one. Each morning and afternoon she arrived at rehearsal in different designer outfits which never failed to catch the eyes of the gentlemen in the orchestra. They were highly amused by the two contrasting types of women: the rich, formida-ble and confident American, expecting to sing with her indis-posed friend, and the down-to-earth girl from Ireland.

On that occasion, I had ten days to learn Hindemith's enthralling opera, sung in German. In it was an exciting race to the finishing line between soprano and contralto, with the stricken Susanna – sung by me – ending on an anguished top C as she is buried alive in a wall. It still gives me claustrophobia to think about it.

As the days wore on I became more and more intimidated by my exalted colleague, who made it known that she thought little of the Irish and their troubled land. It certainly did nothing for my morale, or to ease my fears about possibly missing some top Cs before a live audience. But our lovely engineers, noticing my anxiety, made two, off the cuff, recordings to be inserted at a later date in case of emergency.

When it is not shrouded in mist and fog, Turin is very beautiful, with French – inspired architecture, regal squares and beautiful riverside walks. It is also within easy reach of the lovely Val D'Aosta, where I once joined some Italian friends for a wonderful Christmas in the snow, away from it all. I was afraid to ski, in case I broke my leg, but I enjoyed watching those who were more adventurous. Christmas Eve was sheer magic when my friends and I went to midnight mass in a tiny chapel, down in a valley, beneath a starry sky.

I was so nervous before the concert, which was recorded, that I walked the feet off myself round Turin to get rid of the week's built-up tension. It certainly did the trick, for by the time I reached the radio, I was so pumped up that I didn't need to partake of the bottle of Irish whiskey so kindly, or unkindly, left in my dressing room by my colleague. Just before we made our entrance, she whispered: "Let's face it, honey, your country's finished." "Is it, indeed?" I murmured to myself. It was just the medicine the doctor ordered. I was so mad that I surprised even myself, sailing up and over the top notes, like an Irish mare romping home to the finish in the Grand National.

Just round the corner from the Turin RAI is the imposing Teatro Regio. Even my two contracts to sing there were interrupted when smoke threatened to engulf the building, yet again.

My Viennese pianist and I had already set off for the Piemontese capital feeling decidedly "under the weather". I was desperately trying to throw off the remains of a nasty bout of flu, while Rainer Keuschnig – the fabulous pianist from the Kontrapunckte Ensemble – was trying to prevent one from progressing further.

I was disappointed not to be in good shape to sing glorious music, demanding pathos and desperation, in the second half of a tribute to the German composer Gustav Mahler. Instead of becoming fully immersed in the music, all I could do was to pray that I would survive the evening, let alone deliver.

Turin has many beautiful shops, and to cheer ourselves up we went on a shopping spree, spending money in anticipation of being paid in cash after the concert.

After a hearty lunch, we made our way to the theatre where we were met by the distinct odour of burning rubber exuding from the very stage on which we were to perform. Our rehearsal had to be abandoned when the fumes clogged our nostrils, settling on my vocal chords and obliterating what little voice remained to me following my flu bug. Determined to find the cause of this obnoxious smell, we sniffed round until we came to a screen erected to project slides portraying the life of Mahler. Smoke was belching from it. I completely lost my cool when the management refused to remove the projector, reassuring us that its "teething problems" would subside with time. In the meantime, we would just have to put up with the inconvenience. To add to our distress, we were then informed that, due to a financial crisis – not an unusual occurrence in Italy – we wouldn't be paid until the situation was resolved. Fortunately for us, the Austrian Institute was co-sponsoring the venture and rescued us from an embarrassing situation.

By concert time, the smell of burning rubber had filtered down to the dressing rooms below the stage, where, in between gargling with mineral water, Rainer and I held dampened handkerchiefs over our mouths and noses.

While we were administering such drastic measures to our troubled souls, strains of Mahler's *Kindertoten Lieder* wafted down to us from the exhibition upstairs. We couldn't believe our ears, since we too were going to perform the work in the second half: so why had they played a recording of Dame Janet Baker and the Berlin Philharmonic in the first?

"How am I going to follow such an act?" I wailed to Rainer.

"How am I going to compete on the piano with the Berlin Philharmonic?" said the desperate Rainer.

One of our most memorable duo concerts nearly didn't take place at all. It happened while Rainer Keuschnig and I were on a mini-tour of the Veneto region, when our train was struck by lightning. Naturally, it caused total rail chaos before dropping us off, hours behind schedule, at Padua, our first port of call. There we were to perform at the lovely university where Galileo lectured, and in whose theatre we actually stood.

Just before we were due to leave for the recital our agent told us that, owing to lack of publicity, the following evening's concert at the music conservatoire in nearby Rovigo had to be postponed. All we could do in such a no-win situation was to go back home and return a week later, when, once again, Rainer had to make an overnight journey from Vienna.

I arrived in Rovigo the evening before the concert in order to rest well before such a strenuous programme. Before turning in, I decided to take a stroll around the town, expecting to see posters advertising the event, but found no visible signs of our impending concert anywhere; not even outside the conservatoire where the concert was to take place.

The following day Rainer calmly concluded that perhaps we had got the wrong year! And so, with "to be, or not to be" on our minds, we decided to live dangerously in Rovigo and indulge in a bottle of wine with our lunch – strictly against our pre-concert rules – before setting off for the conservatoire to rehearse.

Although deserted, the building was at least open, albeit without a porter. We found the concert hall at the top of an impressive marble staircase. Once we started to rehearse, I knew that we were going to perform well; the Steinway grand had a glorious tone; the hall was large, with acoustics which would have made anyone sound like Maria Callas.

The rest of that Saturday afternoon was spent wondering if our journey had been really necessary. At nine o'clock we dutifully made our way to the conservatoire, which was still open and fully illuminated, although not a soul was to be seen. At 9.25 pm, five minutes before we were due to start, the situation hadn't changed. Then, just as we were preparing to abandon ship, a man appeared out of the blue, and introduced himself as the director of the conservatoire. Neither Rainer nor I had the courage to ask about the whereabouts of the audience. Suddenly, as if a volcano had erupted, what seemed like the entire population of Rovigo rushed up the stairs to take their seats for the beginning of our concert.

I had been concerned that our chosen programme might be too heavy for such a young audience, many of whom were students at the conservatoire. Instead, they just basked in everything we did, while we gave our all in return. Such a rapport between artists and audience is rare, but we were performing to real music lovers who, it transpired, had been delayed because of a TV transmission of Bizet's Carmen that had nearly clashed with our concert, which they also didn't want to miss.

No story of mine can be complete without mentioning *Amore and Psyche*, a one-act opera composed by my great Sicilian pal, Salvatore Sciarrino. I have yet to encounter anything so difficult, both vocally and theoretically, as this exceptionally challenging work which, written for mezzo-soprano, stretches up and beyond the vocal tessitura.

At that time I was still listed as a soprano with a "good bottom and top" – to the voice that is – but allowed myself to be coaxed into accepting the part when the Italian singer, for whom it was originally written, lost two stone in weight and came out in spots.

When I saw the score I immediately refused to do it. Knowing that I would, Salvo had already plotted how to win me round. After a good, largely liquid lunch in the intense summer heat of Rome, I was lulled and wooed into a state of oblivious acceptance, after Salvo promised to bring down some of the top notes "to a lower shelf" so that I could reach them.

I spent the following busy months learning trills and developing notes – both top and bottom – that I never knew I had, simultaneously fitting everything into a non-stop three beats in the bar. I believe that Psyche was an impressionistic character, but I was so busy coping with her vocal line that I could only think about myself.

"How can you expect a no-nonsense, down-to-earth Ulster woman like me to even *imagine* what an ethereal person like Psyche could be like?" I wailed to Salvo, who took it all in his stride, occasionally reminding me, when I became quite hysterical, that I was the only singer for whom he had had to transpose notes down because I couldn't reach them. Even my friends were beginning to suffer from the effects of the piece when I just couldn't stop counting three beats in a bar. To relieve the tension, a real pal took me to the cinema, but I couldn't concentrate on the film because of the unrelenting rhythms inside my head. Neither could she when my very seat moved to three beats in a bar! At least it proved my theory that muscles automatically remember.

We did have lots of laughs, although the Italian radio did not think it funny when I continued to trill on in full flight, unaware I was three bars out of time with the orchestra. An entire section in the recording had to be repeated, which is forbidden under union rules, while the session was suspended. After an hour, during which I wanted to crawl under the floorboards, an agreement was finally reached. With interminable – typically Italian – arguments, and my nerves in shreds, we spent more than an hour contravening union rules anyway.

In later years, when I was going through a vocal crisis, I discovered that Salvo's writing for mezzo-soprano voice was authentically relevant to that voice's vocal capability. Few singing teachers are aware that a mezzo can actually reach greater heights than a soprano, as long as they don't stay up there too long. Scanning *Amore and Psyche's* vocal ladder was to have a lasting effect both on my voice and entire future, for which I am eternally grateful to Salvo.

Whether it be classical or pop, we all treasure those whom we idolise. Back in my younger days with the Ambrosian Singers in London, I was one of a small group of female singers chosen to sing in a recording of the Debussy *Nocturnes* at the Kingsway Hall. It was just at that time in the late 1960s that the then director of EMI Walter Legge, brought the Italian conductor Carlo Maria Giulini to the fore in many memorable recordings with the Philarmonia Orchestra, of which we were a privileged part.

Giulini, with his halting English and elegant stature, took all the girls' fancies; so much so that we were so weak at the knees that we didn't hear a word he said; instead, we just sat open-mouthed, staring at this gorgeous man.

A decade later, I was a soloist under his direction in Rome, when I just happened to be in the right place at the right time. One morning, while I was walking along a corridor at the RAI headquarters, I bumped into the big chief's right-hand man, Dr Cesare Madzonis – always a great support to me in my career – who said: "Marjorie, could you have a look at the score of *Das Paradies Und Die Peri* by Schumann?" I nearly swooned when he showed me the glorious solo for mezzo-soprano, right in the middle of my voice, where I just love to wallow. Then, not for the first time in Rome, I was told to go home and to wait for developments. Cesare eventually rang with instructions to go immediately to rehearse with Maestro Giulini at the RAI auditorium, where the music would be waiting for me. With hindsight, I must have had a brass neck, sight-reading Schumannn before such a world-famous conductor, but I'd have been crazy to miss an experience of a lifetime.

I have never since participated in such a majestic atmosphere as Giulini created. A man of few words, artists not only respected his great knowledge, but were in awe of his presence. Combined with his interpretation of great music, Carlo Maria Giulini was a force to be reckoned with.

After the concert, I was invited with the star-studded cast to an intimate gathering at which the evening's prima donna was guest of honour. During dinner, one of the assembled company happened to lean across the table to congratulate me on my singing. While I was explaining that I had been practically sight-reading the work, the evening's prima donna, with whom I had sung in my London days, boldly interrupted us: "Oh shut up, Marge," she said. "We all know how you saved the show." Throughout my long career, I could never cope with bitchy female singers like her. They "had me for breakfast", until I grew talons to defend myself. Now I give as good as I get.

The name of the conductor Raphael Kubelik, who died during the writing of this book, is legendary. When I received a telegram at my Roman home, inviting me to sing *Commiato* with him at the Bayerischer Rundfunk – the Bavarian Radio – in Munich, I was over the moon with excitement. As with Giulini, the experience of working with such an international conductor is to be treasured, and Kubelik was no exception.

Not only was it my debut in Germany, but the German premiere of *Commiato*, about which Maestro Dallapiccola was, naturally, rather anxious. He himself wasn't well enough to make the long trip from Florence to Munich, so before I left, I went to Florence to ask if I should write to Herr Kubelik to enquire how he was going to conduct the work. But as neither of us had the courage to ask, we decided to let the matter drop.

I shall never forget my first rehearsal with Herr Kubelik. A man of imposing stature, he greeted me warmly, immediately putting me at my ease by saying: "Would you let me see how you are going to sing this work? You see, you have done it before and I haven't".

Of course, such an experienced conductor knew exactly how he was going to approach it. I often wondered if Maestro Dallapiccola had secretly changed his mind about writing to him about my dilemma.

Munich was a wonderful setting for such a pleasant mission. I was amazed that I could safely wander into a beer house alone, and sit watching the merry Bavarians sing and dance.

The concert hall of the Munich Radio was packed for the concert, which I assumed was being recorded. The first work in the programme by Bruno Maderna was performed without a conductor, so that Herr Kubelik and I were left alone to pace up and down outside the entrance to the stage.

"Terrible this waiting around, isn't it?" he said.

"Yes. I'm a bundle of nerves," I replied.

Suddenly, emerging from a radio beside us were familiar strains, identical to those being played on stage.

"Is it going out live?" I asked Herr Kubelik, trying to hide from him my fear of direct transmissions.

"Yes, and to Spain as well," he replied.

But once on stage, we were off! There are always great moments in one's musical career which cannot be surpassed, and this was one of them. This powerful conductor was so immersed in his work that he just carried me along like a whirlwind in the dramatic parts, and a lark in the more tranquil ones. After I had finished the last top note, when the soloist is left alone, we were both completely drained from all the emotion involved; yet, the unrelenting applause brought us back, and back again.

The critics raved about *Commiato*, and so they should have. In my humble opinion it is one of the finest works ever written.

When I got back to Rome, I had hardly put my key in the lock when the phone rang. "Sono Luigi Dallapiccola." The maestro had the endearing habit of announcing who he was first, but this time he couldn't wait for me to arrive back in Italy with a first-hand account of how his work had been received. When I told him about the prolonged and rapturous applause, he wasn't the least bit impressed.

"Never mind the applause," he said, "I'm more interested in what those beasts (the critics) had to say." There and then, I sent off photocopies of what "the beasts" had said by express delivery to Florence. He was more than delighted.

By sheer coincidence, the Munich concert was dedicated to the memory of Bruno Maderna. I had prolonged the difficult task of writing to his widow Christina, and was more than embarrassed when I found myself sitting beside her at dinner. But once I explained that I hadn't known what to say at the time of his death, she graciously put me at ease by saying, "There is nothing to say."

It was Schubert's beautiful sacred work *Lazurus* that paved my way to La Scala, Milan. The first step was taken in Bologna, one of Italy's most interesting cities, noted for its fine architecture and haute cuisine.

Although I worked with the crème de la crème of Italian musical circles, I did nothing to enhance my career in England when, after a performance in Bologna, the Earl of Harewood – first cousin to Queen Elizabeth 11 – visited us backstage.

A Scottish friend had made a special pilgrimage to Bologna to hear me perform some classical music – for a change – and to sample some wonderful Bolognese delicacies. When he realised that we were all going out to dinner in such distinguished company, he delivered a warning: "Marge, do be careful what you say, and please don't drink any wine, or you'll start sneezing."

All went well until Lord Harewood graciously turned round to me and asked what I was going to sing the following season. Unaware that he had hit a nerve, and stimulated by mineral water only, I took off.

"I'm trying to learn Britten's *The Turn of the Screw*", I said, "and *Elegy For Young Lovers* by Hans Werner Henze. Both are in Italian, and are driving me insane. In my opinion, opera should not be performed outside its original language." As if enough hadn't been said, I added, "It totally distorts the notes and the vowel sounds. It's like singing Wagner in English, instead of German."

There was such a hush all round that I knew I had put my foot right in it. The gentleman to whom I had addressed this oration just happened to be the director of the English National Opera, where everything at that time, was sung in English, including

Wagner's *Ring Cycle*.

My friend said nothing on the way back to my hotel, until he could no longer refrain from "letting me have it".

"What did you think you were doing, Marge," he cried, "trying to commit professional suicide?"

Of course he was right, since even I knew that I had well and truly cooked my goose. Since then I have considerably mellowed in the faux pas department, and try to take stock of my surroundings before uttering. After one famous gaffe at a dinner party in Stockholm, a desperate colleague begged me to "open my mouth for singing purposes only".

One of my luckiest places is the concert hall of Milan's Conservatoire of Giuseppe Verdi. Its spacious auditorium is home to prestigious concerts given by the RAI and the Pomeriggi Musicali, for whom I sang music of every imaginable type, from Wagner's *Wesendonck Lieder* to the latest editions, straight off the press. We performed *Lazurus* there, immediately after Bologna, and it attracted more than favourable press notices. By sheer good luck, they were read by Sylvano Bussotti, the famous Italian avant-garde composer, who was looking for a robust soprano to sing the role of Vittoria Colonna – the spiritual mistress of Michelangelo – in his new opera, *Nottetempo*, to be premiered at La Scala, Milan. Ornella, our mutual agent, mentioned my name to him, before negotiating a contract for me with the most famous opera house in the world. Amazingly, I didn't have to audition for what was to be the most traumatic experience of my life.

It is not unusual for a brand new opera to be behind schedule, so you can imagine the state of my nerves when I arrived at La Scala for the first rehearsal with only one completed page of the one-act opera. We learnt it, with the help of a superhuman repetiteur, as it came off the press, and was immediately delivered to us by couriers. For the ensuing week our lives were transformed into a pattern of study, sleep and eating, while our daily musical packets continued to arrive from the publishers. When a friend rang my B&B to speak to me, he was informed by the protective landlady that the Signorina Wright was unavailable, because she had been up all night studying.

One morning I bumped into my bass colleague who, like me,

liked to walk round the precincts of La Scala searching for his "system" – in other words, trying to work out a method to place the notes in the voice.

"I don't see the composer around," he said.

"No you won't," I informed him. "He's still composing!"

In the meantime, I was sure the Italian police would arrest me for disturbing the peace, since I walked round the street struggling to reach some excruciatingly high notes. I suppose they had become used to highly-strung singers livening up that area.

No operatic tale would be complete without the usual metaphorical scratching out of eyes amongst the prima donnas. There were three sopranos in the cast, with me in the unenviable position of being caught in the middle of a feud between the other two. Apparently, it had originated in Vienna, after one of them had been selected in favour of the other for the part of *Lulu* in Berg's sexy opera about a prostitute. I could see why. The successful one was both beautiful and sweet, while the other, not so affable soprano, was more robust. She was also a ruthless opponent of anyone who took work from Italian nationals and, to the best of my knowledge, was one of the instigators of my removal from the Italian musical scene. Though she did get her comeuppence when she went on a tour of Asia, under the supervision of my Italian friend, Gabriella Ponte, who was her guide. Naturally, when Gabriella heard that she had a prima donna on board, she asked her if she knew me. Apparently, the reply was less than savoury; it must have been, because my friend couldn't repeat what had been said, although I imagined the script.

Just before my diva colleague left her home in Florence to go on the trip, she dreamt that her mink coat had been stolen. Taking care that this didn't happen in her absence, she took the coat with her on the Asian tour. Unfortunately, her dream came all too true when the coat was stolen in Thailand, and not in Italy, leaving poor Gabriella to deal with operatic histrionics and ramifications surrounding the incident. "Serves you right," she thought to herself, "for all the nasty things you said about Marge."

While we were rehearsing at La Scala, the Royal Opera House were performing there. The company included my friend and compatriot Heather Harper and Dame Janet Baker. It gave

Heather and me a great chance to catch up on home gossip and polish up our Ulster accents.

This period also coincided with St. Patrick's Day, when I couldn't resist an invitation to an Irish party in Milan. At last I was able to let my hair down and get away from the mounting tension, as countdown to the new production loomed at the opera house. Next morning, as I answered the early morning call from La Scala, I wished that I hadn't drunk so many Irish coffees and gins, especially when yet another unseen piece of the score appeared at the rehearsal.

The day of the dress rehearsal and press preview is imprinted in my memory. The first ominous signs of trouble appeared in the shape of another "ugly sister", who had not been chosen to sing in our opera. It was well known that she too was out for my blood because I had taken work from an Italian national. She also had strong contacts in the right places, causing concern for my survival among my lovely and loyal Italian colleagues, who warned me to stay well clear of her talons.

That same evening, the sombre-faced administrator of the Piccola Scala, the Scala's smaller theatre, came to see me in my dressing room, where he told me that he had bad news for me. I nearly died of shock, for I had received news that very morning that my elderly mother had been operated on, back home in Newry. Since I had no understudy, I was legally forced to ride out the Milan performances until I was able to fly home to her. I heaved a sigh of relief that the "devastating news" was that I was to be replaced by an Italian national at a concert at the Piccola Scala. The lame excuse was that the Questura, the foreigner's department of the Italian police, had refused to grant me a work permit. Next morning, smelling a rat and realising that the worms were crawling out of the woodwork, I decided to get to the root of the matter. I had already deduced that in no way, by EEC law, could the Italian police have refused me permission to work. So off I went to the Questura, where my entrance was greeted with utter amazement.

"Why aren't you resting for the opening tonight?" the clerks asked.

"Because I want to see your director."

Of course they were right. I should have been relaxing; instead there I was demanding to see the head of the Questura, who was both charming and attentive.

"I am a member of the European Community. Why won't you give me a work permit for the concert?" I demanded.

"Because La Scala didn't ask for one," he amazingly revealed.

When the concert did take place, no one was surprised when I was replaced by the soprano who had appeared at the dress rehearsal. She also got her comeuppence when, as she was getting out of her car, on her way into the theatre, she jammed her thumb in its front door, leaving her with a bandaged hand to enhance her designer outfit. Once again, my Italian spies in the audience were reminded that "it doesn't do to meddle with Marge".

Although I had many enemies, I also had lots of friends. The Italian music establishment has always been my great benefactor, and I shall be eternally grateful to them for all that they did for me. Not only did they "adopt me" as one of their own but treated me like a princess. My bond with Italy will never be broken.

The first night of the opera was postponed because of a strike – part of the Italian norm – but when it did take off, we encountered amazing scenes. The Italian public had wanted to hear Puccini or Verdi, and were indignant that financial cuts had been made to accommodate the Bussotti production, while reducing expenditure on a visit to Washington by the resident La Scala company. They booed and hissed throughout the entire opera, creating conditions under which it was nearly impossible to sing, let alone be heard. The only one to whom they listened was me; not because I was better than my colleagues, but, by a stroke of luck, the first word in my aria happened to be the Italian word for silence, which I "socked" to them.

After the ordeal, while my soprano colleague and I were having our wigs removed, she unexpectedly turned round to me and said, "Was that the first time you've been booed and hissed?"

"Yes," I answered defiantly.

"Oh, I'm quite used to it," she proudly admitted.

After the last performance, I flew home to Ireland to the bedside of my sick mum, who survived to share more adventurous stories with me. While they helped to keep her alive, they nearly finished off her daughter.

Alas, Rome was too inconveniently located for my professional commitments, so I decided to move to Milan, where overnight trains to Vienna and other European capitals were more accessible.

I hated leaving my many friends, and all the wonderful parties to which I was invited. But we still have our memories, outstanding among which is the unforgettable Christmas we foreigners, who were unable to get home, spent there. It started off with a wine and cheese party I gave on Christmas Eve, during which I had to pop round to the baker's nearby to baste the turkey he was roasting for me in his oven for the next day. After the party we all went to St. Peter's Square to take part in the poignant inauguration of Holy Year. Then, on Christmas night we transported a sherry trifle I had made to a friend's party, unaware that my cleaning lady had dusted some foreign coins into the bag in which the trifle was being carried. It was only when one of the guests took a German pfennig out of his mouth that I realised something was wrong. While I stood gaping at him in horror, our host charmingly assured the victim that it was an English tradition to place coins in Christmas puddings! Next day, when I rang the unfortunate victim to apologise, his wife said: "Oh don't worry about killing him off darling; I've been trying to get rid of him for years!"

Had I known that the move northwards was to be the beginning of instability on the domestic front, I might have thought twice about leaving such an intimate and socially inclined environment for a more business-like one. It certainly was a major turning point in my life.

In the meantime, I soldiered on, returning to Vienna to rejoin the Kontrapunckte Ensemble for the first time in Vienna since we rehearsed *Commiato* there. The reason for my visit was to sing Bruno Maderna's one-act opera *Hyperion*, in concert version, at the famous and wonderful Musikverein. This imposing concert hall is world famous. The home of the Vienna Philharmonic Orchestra, this ochre and gold sala, surrounded by imposing columns, is the familiar venue for the annual New Year's Day concert, which is televised worldwide. One morning, when Rainer Keuschnig and I were passing by the great hall, on our way to practice in one of the rooms, we caught a rare glimpse of Herbert von Karajan, eyes closed, rehearsing the famous Vienna Philharmonic.

It had been arranged for me to go Florence, after the concert, to rehearse with Luigi Dallapiccola, who, for the first time, was to conduct *Commiato* at the conservatoire in Turin. I was astounded and shocked when, just before I left for the Musikverein, I happened to turn on the radio, from which news of Luigi Dallapiccola's sudden death was being relayed. Not only was it a personal and professional blow for me, but a weird coincidence that I happened to be back in Vienna for the first time since performing the world premiere of *Commiato* with the Kontrapunckte. I was also singing a piece by Bruno Maderna, the composer at whose memorial concert I had performed Dallapiccolas's masterpiece in Munich.

That night it was a case of the "show must go on". But as the terrible news of Dallapiccola's death – which I had brought with me – quickly spread, a great sadness cast its shadow over the performance.

Back in Italy, it had been decided to go ahead with the Turin concert under the direction of a brilliant young Florentine conductor, Massimo de Bernard. It was tough going, singing *Commiato* on such an emotional occasion, especially a work in which the composer had seen his own "Abschied", meaning "farewell" in German. Not only was it a fitting conclusion to my Dallapiccola era, but a turning point, which nearly brought my career to a halt.

Chapter 6

Tremors

It's not every day a singer flies in to Venice to sing at La Fenice encased in a surgical collar. It certainly caused quite a stir, since all those concerned wondered how I was going to perform after a car crash in Belfast, from which my cousin and I miraculously escaped. She emerged unscathed, while I had a sprained ankle, coupled with a severe attack of whiplash.

"You must have nine lives," was all our gallant rescuer could say, as he helped us out of the car after it had been hit – side on – from a vehicle emerging at speed from a side road. By sheer good luck there were no passengers in the back seats, which were a right-off, while the front two remained intact.

The Venetians panicked when they saw the collar, but I immediately reassured them that the voice was in working order. I would be able to sing the soprano part in Stravinsky's *Les Noces* which, fortunately for me, was a ballet with four singers and two pianists, all of whom were accommodated in the orchestral pit. I had to remove the surgical collar to sing, but must admit that I enjoyed the sympathy it brought me from the warm-hearted Venetians, who applauded my *corragio* on performing a work which I loved, and for which I was being well paid.

Les Noces was fraught with tension from day one. Word circulated round the theatre that the Swiss conductor was depending on me, with my reputation for "infallibility", to hold the rocky quartet of ill-chosen singers together. May I explain that Stravinsky's music is so rhythmically complicated that if a beat is missed disaster strikes; which is exactly what happened.

The opening night at La Fenice was packed out. All went well until our unstable quartet reached a crucial point in the work, just before the entrance of the chorus. To my horror, I felt a certain parting of the vocal ways with my mates in the lower regions, as I hung on to my note on the top line and hoped for the best. When I glanced up at the conductor, all I could see was his icy glare. He was evidently blaming me for the missed beat. Miraculously, the wizard chorus-master, who later solved my own vocal problems, rallied his group to attack in the right place and prevent a calamity.

We received a rapturous ovation. No one, besides ourselves, was aware of the mishap until the conductor publicly attacked me at the side of the stage.

"What did you think you were doing?" he roared.

"There were three other soloists singing with me, so don't blame me for other's mistakes", I said, rallying to my own defence.

I hardly slept that night, next door to the conductor's room. Through its paper-thin walls, I listened to the story of how I had ruined his performance being narrated by phone to all those who must not have relished being woken from their sleep.

Early next morning, I rang my agent in Rome to get my end of the story in first. The conductor must have overheard me, since he later said, "You're like a press office next door; I hardly got a wink of sleep because of your chatter!"

The story didn't end there. The Italian mezzo-soprano objected to my getting favourable write-ups in Italian newspapers, while she wasn't even mentioned. The *post mortem* took place in the lounge of the Taverna La Fenice Hotel, where the conductor and I were attempting to repair the damage after the previous night's mishap. Suddenly, our mezzo-soprano colleague, armed with newspapers, swooped down on me in a torrent of rage.

"I am a great singer," she cried, "while she is at the beginning of her career."

At this point, even the conductor's jaw had opened considerably wider, as our angry colleague continued: "I'll have you know", she declared, glaring at me like an animal about to devour its prey, "that I have sung Stravinsky with Pierre Boulez."

"I'll have you know, that I have sung Stravinsky with Stravinsky," I announced triumphantly, before sweeping out of the lounge like a temperamental diva.

Later, the conductor, consumed with curiosity about the authenticity of my performing with the great composer enquired, "Did you really sing with Stravinsky?"

"Yes," I truthfully replied. What I didn't tell him was that I had sung in a performance of his *Persephone* when I was filling in as an extra in the BBC chorus, back in London.

The following day another performance and missed beats loomed before us. That morning, when I went for a trip on a motor boat to get away from the scene of the crime, I bumped into some of the female chorus.

"It was the moment to stop!" they hissed together, like Rhine maidens rising out of the Grand Canal.

That evening, as I was leaving the hotel to warm up in the theatre, who should show up but my tenor and bass colleagues, who had taken their convenient leave of Venice after the first performance. Refreshed and smiling, they casually enquired, "Any write-ups? Any new developments during our absence?"

Guessing from our icy silence and blank expressions that all was not well, the tenor said, "Oh come on, Wright, I have plenty of work, and so have you. What does it matter what a critic says about us?"

Just then, the conductor and the mezzo also emerged *en route* for the theatre. Once the story of my missed beat had been raised, the bass, who usually played comic roles, burst out laughing.

"I was the culprit" he nobly confessed. "If it hadn't been for Wright holding on like grim death to her top note until I got back on track, the whole performance would have collapsed."

That evening, in the foyer of Albergo La Fenice where, as you might have guessed by now, the off-stage drama was nearly more exciting than that in the adjoining opera house, I knew what it must feel like to be acquitted.

In the spring of 1976 I was back again at La Fenice, singing in Dallapiccola's oratorio *Job*. I was honoured to be a part of this stage adaptation, doubling up as the Messenger who brings woeful tidings to Job. When I took part in a concert version of the opera at Santa Cecilia, there was a Polish narrator who left us spellbound after his luscious tones delivered a spine-chilling warning of impending doom. Often a foreign accent can turn even such a wonderful language as Italian into something really special. However, he was unable to accept the Venice contract and was replaced by an Italian singer. However, the poor man discovered that the spoken word required a certain amount of skill, which he tried to master as he walked round Venice, agonising at the thought of the looming first night. As I tried to reassure him that all would be well on the night, little did I imagine that one day I too would be pacing round that romantic city in a similar state.

The great big thorn in my flesh was the producer, a minute lady, who happened to be the daughter of one of Italy's most powerful impresarios, a man who had always treated me with kindness and respect.

Each rehearsal was a nightmare, when the producer and repetiteur attacked my voice, my appearance and my Italian pronunciation, until Oslavio Decredico, one of Italy's leading tenors in the field of contemporary music, rescued me. Tired of the persistent interruptions, he ordered everyone, including the producer and the conductor to keep quiet while he gave me the singing lesson of my life. Before everyone he ordered me to drop my jaw down, and then use my tongue to pronounce the tricky Italian consonants, which had plagued me for years. The production ran smoothly, my vocal problems having been solved by the wonderful Oslavio, until my next on-stage encounter with the producer.

My dramatic entrance, bearing news of Job's terrible plight, was to be made through a hole in the scenery at the back of the stage. Numerous attempts were made to get me through it, to coincide with the first beat of the bar. The conductor despaired at yet another missed beat, and one of the theatre's repetiteurs was employed to perch me on a step and push me through the treacherous hole, which I knew was too small for me.

In a desperate attempt to reach a compromise, I suggested that the producer, in calculating the hole's measurements, had taken her own tiny form into consideration, instead of my larger one.

"You try getting through that hole," I challenged her. She did, but only just.

"If you can't, then how can I?" I demanded. Mercifully, the hole was sufficiently enlarged to enable me to deliver my news about Job on time. We all heaved a sigh of relief when the producer and coaches departed after the first night, which nearly didn't take place at all.

During our rehearsal period it became unusually warm and humid in Venice, even for May. One unforgettable day was particularly still and atmospheric, disturbed only by the uncanny barking of dogs and wailing of cats. That evening, I had just paid the bill in a restaurant near St. Mark's Square, when I felt and heard what I thought was an explosion. Having just flown in from Ulster, my immediate reaction was to take to my heels, as water surged under my feet and buildings rocked. I followed hordes of screaming people into the Square, where I ran into Oslavio Decredico who, apart from his singing talent, is also an expert on earth-quakes. As I followed his weather forecasts over the ensuing days, I felt I was becoming one, too!

It transpired that we had just been at the epicentre of the terrible earthquake that had devoured nearby Friuli. Only the sea and sand, which apparently absorb shock, had saved lovely Venice from destruction. As we sat in the St. Mark's Square, Oslavio asked me if I could swim.

"Only a little," I replied.

"You hang onto me," he said confidently, "I'm a champion."

Only then did it dawn on me that there we were stranded on a lagoon on which we could be marooned.

The first impact had taken place at 9.30 pm, and at 11 pm we made out way back to the hotel, where people were packing, ready to escape. The tremor had occurred during the interval of an opera at La Fenice, just as the cast were descending the stairs leading to the stage.

"I want Mamma," cried a light soprano, who was immediately landed a controlling smack by her more formidable and loud-voiced female colleague. Meanwhile, back at the hotel, Oslavio was forecasting another tremor for 1.30 am; and sure enough there was. It had us all leaping out of our beds and down to the foyer, where the keys shook behind the reception desk.

"The next one will be at 5 am," announced our weather fore-caster who, as you can imagine, was not too popular with the manager when even more frightened guests considered vacating their rooms for safer regions. As we were under contract, we had to stay put until the theatre was examined for damage. Fortunately for us, only the facade was slightly affected, enabling us to carry on with our schedule. An earthquake is considered to be an "act of God", and therefore would have exonerated the theatre from financial liabilities for lost hotel and restaurant bills, for which we would have to dig deep into our pockets.

All the ensuing musical changes in my life seemed to involve Venice and La Fenice. The dramatic and poignant music of Dallapiccola, as well as Sciarrino's *Amore and Psyche,* had stretched my voice to unimaginable dimensions. But I still hadn't found the teacher who could really solve my vocal problems, until one day a friend of Aldo Danieli, the brilliant chorus master at La Fenice, invited him and one or two of the cast from *Job* to have after-lunch drinks with him in his beautiful apartment on the Grand Canal.

After a few "jars" we all began to sing without inhibitions. I was well away, in true Irish style, until I was stopped in my tracks by Aldo who, detecting an unfamiliar ring to my voice, produced, from nowhere, an aria antica which, being written in a comfort-able, but lower key, admirably suited me. Everyone was thrilled to hear my "real" voice as we went back to the theatre, singing our heads off. Aldo's impromptu lesson had given me food for thought, so that a new sound emerged from my throat at the fol-lowing evening's performance, setting me free to portray Dallapiccola's work with the inner depth which it demanded.

During one of my treasured consultations with Luigi Dallapiccola, he was curious to know how I warmed up my voice. I told him that I used Verdi and Puccini arias.

"There are only three people who know how to write about the voice," he said. "Verdi, Puccini and myself." Please don't think that he was being arrogant, since I totally agreed with him. Those composers who do accommodate singers' voices are few and far between.

The first signs of vocal trouble appeared during rehearsals for the opening of the 1976/1977 season at La Fenice. I was thrilled when I was invited to sing Bruno Maderna's one-act opera *Hyperion* on this glittering occasion, imagining it to be a piece of cake, after singing it with ease at Bruno's memorial concert in Vienna, where the space and acoustics of the Musikverein enhanced the extremely high notes.

I was to work on this piece with the same conductor in the *Les Noces* episode, along with Virginio Puercher, a noted Italian producer, who not only liked to shock his public but make dramatic last-minute changes to the production.

Hyperion only took up part of the inaugural programme, so the conductor had other seemingly more important issues on his mind. Owing to a shortage of orchestral rehearsals, my singing and movements had to be co-ordinated with a tape recording of a German soprano, who had a much lighter voice than mine. The theory that muscles remember was worthily proved in this instance, as mine became so used to this sound, beautiful as it may have been, that I just couldn't imagine using my own voice again. As the days wore on, I became so inhibited from being forbidden to sing the work in my own voice, that my throat seized up from sheer fright to the point of transmitting my terror to those around me. My only other colleague in this bizarre production was the revered Severino Gazzeloni, one of Italy's finest flautists. He simply loved my Irish pronunciation of his name and, considering his fame, was a dear to work with, when he wasn't commuting to Rome to support his favourite football team.

My out-of-character silence and solitary walks round Venice had not gone unnoticed by those in daily contact with me, not least Aldo Danieli who stopped me in my tracks outside the theatre.

"What on earth is wrong with you, Marjorie?" he asked. "You're no longer the laughing, happy girl we all know."

It was the moment for me to confide in someone that I simply couldn't sing the piece. My voice had acquired a new depth as a result of singing heavier and more demanding roles. My biggest mistake was in accepting the Maderna work in the first place.

Aldo lost no time in marching me into La Fenice, where he cleverly divided my voice into different sections to enable me to get up and down the vocal ladder without strangling myself. It was not only masterly coaching, but immediately effective.

Eventually, and dangerously close to opening night, we were transferred to the theatre to become acquainted with the orchestra and stage manoeuvres. To describe them as bizarre is an understatement. Instead of walking onto the stage, I had to approach it from the basement where a group of lovely men helped me to stand on a tiny, specially made platform, which was then pulled up by ropes onto the stage, like a phoenix rising out of the ashes. Then, with my knees hurting like hell, I had to sing exceptionally high notes while crawling towards the conductor and audience over an iron grill. After I complained, a pair of cricket pads appeared which, although they impeded my progress, were preferable to bleeding knees.

There were more problems when a residue of dust, left behind after the platform took off from its "launching pad", affected my voice. As a remedy, the stage hands in the "lower regions" brought bottles of delicious white wine to the dress rehearsal to wash away the dust from our lungs. By the time "blast off" arrived, I was so merry that I don't know how I didn't fall off the platform and kill myself.

Sure enough, on opening night, Virginio lived up to his reputation when he made me wear a heavy military great coat – I was supposed to be a lonely warrior – draped over my shoulders. It took courage to walk out of my dressing room that night when even my front teeth had been blackened out. I was lucky to get away with it, since singing a work beyond one's vocal capability is inviting trouble. After such a bitter lesson, I knew that *Hyperion* was my swan song as a high soprano.

My Venetian sojourn ended just in time for Christmas. I was glad to get back to my friends in Milan, for, although Venice is the most beautiful place on earth, it can be lonely and dismal in winter, with high tides disrupting mobility on land and water. Another soprano and I made a dramatic exit from the city on top of our porters' trolleys, before they deposited us, along with our luggage, on a boat. I found it hilarious, but my colleague thought it was no way to treat two prima donnas.

Christmas of 1997 was spent in the lovely Val D'Aosta with

some German friends, who traditionally celebrated the feast on Christmas Eve. Unfortunately, I had to leave for Turin on St. Stephen's night, not having completely memorised the enormous score of Hans Werner Henze's *Elegy For Young Lovers*, translated, for the first time, into Italian from W. H. Auden's English text.

I was to sing the part of an eccentric and menopausal Baroness, which suited me right down to the ground, because it was for mezzo-soprano. Although it was wonderful to be finally vocally comfortable, I had problems memorising the Italian text, which in no way corresponded with the original metre of the English one.

The gentleman responsible for this wonderful opportunity to sing with my real voice was the Italian conductor Gianpiero Taverna, hero of our stormy opening night at La Scala who, during the weathering of many musical dramas together, had already detected this quality in my voice.

The production of *Elegy For Young Lovers* was fraught from day one. The Italian conductor Nino Sanzogno, with whom I was so much looking forward to working, had suffered a stroke in Chicago, and was replaced at short notice by the intrepid resident conductor of the Teatro Regio, who spent an exhausting Christmas studying a score which he had never before conducted. The next victim was the producer, with whom we had an inspiring first rehearsal, until he also succumbed to a viral infection. He, in turn, was replaced by an even more courageous substitute who, being essentially a prose producer, had produced only one opera in his entire life.

In such hair-raising circumstances, we had just two weeks to get the show off the ground at Teatro Regio in icy, snowbound Turin. I couldn't help comparing the preparation of this production with another more leisurely and summery one at Glyndebourne, in the English countryside. They just couldn't have worked as hard as we did, leaving our hotel at the crack of dawn to warm up in the theatre, which we left at 10 pm to snatch our first meal of the day.

Lack of time forced us to abandon normal piano rehearsal, and we went straight into stage and orchestral production, with the producer shouting instructions from the stalls through a loud hailer. This was extremely effective until the orchestral musicians complained that they couldn't hear themselves play. While all this was going on I was left stranded on the stage with an old-fashioned medicine bag.

"What shall I do with this?" I called out to the stalls.

"Kick it," shouted the producer.

I obeyed his instructions implicitly, giving the bag such a kick that its contents were strewn all over the stage.

"Viva Irlanda," yelled an off-stage coach, as if we were at a football international.

All hell broke loose. The furious producer made his way to the stage shouting: "I'll thank you to leave your Irish sense of humour off-stage." He obviously thought I was "taking the mickey" out of him.

"I would never insult a producer, especially you who are doing such a splendid job," I wailed, to loud cheers all round as the compliment was immediately reciprocated, and the incident brought to a close with hugs and kisses in abundance.

The composer, Hans Werner Henze, a most charming and cultured man, arrived for the dress rehearsal, where he made an unforgettable last-minute change to the production. Throughout the rehearsals I had been told to strike an imitation German clock on a wall, just before the introduction to my big final-act aria, behind which a young stage-hand stood with a gong, poised for action. The change of plan meant that, instead of striking the gong, which represented the clock, after the orchestra had started the introduction to my aria, he had to do it before.

On opening night, before a distinguished and packed house, I dutifully pretended to strike the clock, but the supposedly synchronised response from behind the wall didn't come; in other words, the clock didn't strike! The young man had obviously forgotten about the alteration.

It was a singer's nightmare as I just stood there alone, save for my American bass colleague, seated in the shadows of the massive stage who nonchalantly whispered: "Honey, just keep going. I'm only glad I'm not in your shoes." In the meantime, I had no other option but to make up my own scenes until the conductor began my aria.

I ran to the prompter's box at the front of the stage slightly guarded in my steps, since I could hardly move in the tight skirt I was wearing. He assured me that I had sung everything. I was already aware of that, because I have a photographic memory, which saved my professional skin that night. Fortunately my role of the Baroness was a neurotic one, so that it looked as if it were just a part of the opera when I ran over to my American colleague.

"Just keep on goin', honey," he said in his deep American drawl.

After an eternity and frantic gesturing to the conductor, who just stared at me, I made an effective movement with my larynx, which brought him to his senses, and attacked.

The next day, we ran into each other out shopping.

"What happened?" I asked him.

"Nothing," he replied" I had never seen you act before, I thought you were wonderful."

"*That* was for real!" I told him.

They say things happen in threes; and the third mishap in this story was the most dramatic. The opera opens with an aria sung by a light soprano, while the Baroness sits in the shadow writing at her desk.

With first-night nerves behind us, there was more time to relax and take note of the goings on. Only then did I notice that while Emilia Ravaglia, my petite colleague, was blissfully singing away, a candle was burning dangerously close to the floor-length nylon veil attached to her hair. Next morning, I brought up the subject of the veil with the wardrobe mistress, since I didn't want to unduly frighten Emilia.

"Don't worry, it will be fine," she assured me; but in my bones, I felt disaster ahead. Sure enough, my fears became real at the next performance, which happened to be a packed Sunday matinee. To my horror, a gentle breeze which I had dreaded, plus a step taken back in the wrong direction, set my friend alight. I imagined what it must have been like for Joan of Arc at the stake. While she sang on, blissfully unaware of what was happening, the prompter screamed at her, "You're burning, you're burning." In the meantime, I was up and off my chair, running towards the poor girl as fast as I could in my ridiculously tight skirt. The audience thought it was all part of the opera, until the orchestra stopped playing. By that time I had helped my friend pull off the burning material, before tugging her away from yet another piece of flammable veil. The off-stage fire brigade were soon on the scene and nearly extinguished the lot of us, after which, to a great ovation, we went on with the show in a daze.

The next day, the Italian press released the exaggerated story of how an Irish mezzo-soprano had saved an Italian soprano's life!

It was a treat to get back to my lovely flat in Milan, situated near La Scala, in the artistic Brera quarter, with fine galleries, gourmet restaurants and the lovely church of San Marco where Verdi's *Requiem* was first performed.

I lived in an absolute haven at the top of an apartment block, overlooking the rooftops of Milan, from where I could hear that magical ringing of Italian church bells.

Many a good party I held there for my English colleagues visiting La Scala, or singing at the Radio, so "dropping in on Marge" was a must. Over haute cuisine, I spent hours reminiscing with my old friends, the tenors Philip Langridge and Gerald English, about our early days in London, as Gerry was a connoisseur of food. On one of Gerry's visits He and I took part in a memorable concert version of Schoenberg's *Moses and Aaron*, in which I sang the part, *fully clad*, of second naked virgin, and which I never lived down after it was broadcast to the nation announcing me as "Seconda Vergine Nuda!" Italian announcers experienced great difficulty in pronouncing my first name, varying from Maryioriee to Margarine; but at least it was better than Marge.

In contrast to Rome, where the foreign and diplomatic communities are more prone to congregate, I mainly associated with Italians, with whom I formed lasting friendships. Alas, the Milanese climate is not typically Italian. The air is polluted, the winter is notoriously foggy, while the summer is hot and dirty, especially in August when the Milanese escape to the sea.

Milan was more difficult for foreigners to live in than Rome, and many a visit was made to the Questura to fight for my legal battles, which I invariably won. It was in this gloomy foreigners' office that, on one hot summer's day, I had the most embarrassing experience of my life.

I had recently bought a light pair of old-fashioned shoes from a friend's second-hand shop and decided to impress my interrogators by wearing them. Just as I had proved my point and was about to make a grand exit, I suddenly felt my feet and shoes parting company; the heat had melted the glue between the soles and uppers, leaving me to walk home barefoot. In reality, the Questura clerks were always very nice to me, and often attended the concerts for which they had given me permission to sing.

The area where I lived was full of buzz, right in the middle of exclusive Milanese streets with all those wonderful fashion houses. It was also within walking distance of the Conservatoire of Giuseppe Verdi, where I gave many memorable concerts singing beautiful and interesting music for the Radio and the Pomeriggi Musicali, with whom I had many last-minute adventures, when I often deputised at short notice. It was during preparation for a Sunday evening concert there that I got the fright of my life.

I was sure that I had studied all the required programme, until I happened to glance at a poster in a Milan street where, to my horror, my name was beside a work which I didn't even know. Normally, the music is sent to me by the organisation, but I hadn't received it. Someone had blundered; but I was without a leg to stand on, for the title of the piece was written into the contract, which I had not thoroughly read. There was nothing to do but to forget recriminations and learn the music.

Gianpiero Taverna was conducting, so at least I was with a friend. He explained the idiom of the German piece to me, entitled *Kabaret*, which gave us a certain amount of freedom. I virtually "hammed" my way through the work, which was a roaring success. Nobody knew but us; not even a German friend who complimented me on my pronunciation of her native tongue. I may have learnt how to fool an audience, but I never want to repeat the experience.

It was during these happy times in Milan that I resumed my college friendship with my compatriot James Galway. When he discovered from our mutual friend, Derek Bell – whom he happened to meet again while working together with the Chieftains – that I was within easy reach of his home in Lucerne, he immediately invited me to spend a wonderful weekend with his family beside the lake.

My next visit to the Galways was under rather different circumstances. It was to bring some Italian cheer to Jimmy, recovering in a clinic from his horrendous road accident.

It so happened that my visit coincided with that of Gloria Hunniford, who was interviewing Jimmy on behalf of BBC Northern Ireland. Jimmy, thinking that two birds could be killed with one stone, set up an interview for me with Gloria in her hotel, which was transmitted back home on her successful radio show, *A Taste of Honey*. The noise was so overpowering in her bedroom, however, that we transferred ourselves to the hotel's staircase, where the recording was made. Years later, when I met up with Gloria for a cuppa at the BBC in London, I was amazed when she reminded me of the incident, considering the number of people she had met in the intervening years.

I was heartbroken when I was forced to leave my lovely home in 1978, after a rent act was introduced whereby a tenant could be evicted if the apartment was needed for a family member. It meant that renting other accommodation was virtually impossible. There and then, I had to pack my bags and move my belongings to the headquarters of the generous Autunno Musicale in Como, where I taught singing.

I still yearned for the mountains beside water that I left behind in Ireland, and so, with its similar scenery, I decided to look for a flat in Como. Like Warrenpoint, which is near the border with the Irish Republic, Como is just "down the road" from Lugano, in Switzerland.

In the meantime, I stayed at a lovely lakeside hotel, in true Anita Brookner *Hotel du Lac* style, with facilities to study at the Bossi Academy. It may sound idyllic, but it cost me a fortune while I frantically searched for a home of my own. At last, after months of living this way, a friend in Milan heard that a flat was to let near Milan Central station. Two distinguished Italian musicians came with me as guarantors when I went to meet the landlord and his wife. The contract for the noisy, dingy accommodation was to be signed on my arrival next day, but it never materialised. My friends and I were all so glad that I had finally found a home, that, without considering the consequences, a sigh of relief was expressed all round.

The final act of my story begins from that moment.

During this unsettled spell, I was invited to sing the part of the governess in an Italian translation of Benjamin Britten's, *The Turn of the Screw* adapted from Henry James's enthralling novel.

There had already been signs of trouble, earlier revealed in Venice, when I happened to bump into the Venetian conductor Ettore Gracis, who was to direct the Britten opera. I had worked with him on a previous occasion on amicable, if not communicative terms, since he struck me as being a reserved person who would not have appreciated my chatter.

After formal greetings, I expressed my delight at the thought of our working together again in Genoa, especially as Virginio Puecher, with whom I was currently working, was to produce the Britten opera.

If I had given Ettore Gracis the news that the world was coming to an end, it couldn't have had a more disastrous impact.

"I told them that I didn't want you," he said. "You are too English and stiff to play the part. Britten should be like Puccini, apart from the fact that you are too inexperienced".

I couldn't believe what I was hearing, considering that I was about to open the season at La Fenice. Moreover, Benjamin Britten raised no objection to my being Irish when I worked with him in my days with the Ambrosian Singers.

After this disturbing encounter, I talked to Virginio Puecher who reassured me that, having signed the contract, everything would go according to plan. And so, with uncertain undercurrents, I set out for Genoa on 18th March, sadly refusing an invitation to a tempting St. Patrick's night "hooley" so that I might be refreshed and ready for impending difficulties.

Our first rehearsal with the pianist and conductor went very well, with my lovely Italian colleagues putting me at my ease by paying me undeserved compliments, although they could also have imagined me in the more mature role of the housekeeper, Mrs Grose.

The following morning, we were not only joined by the producer, Virginio Puecher, but by his assistant, who just happened to be the daughter of Ettore Gracis, our conductor. This matey ensemble had previously collaborated in a production of the Britten opera at La Piccola Scala with an Italian soprano, who "conveniently" found herself free to sing my part in Genoa. In order to get rid of me, they found fault with everything I did, much to the embarrassment of the rest of the cast, who suffered on my behalf.

At the end of the gruelling ordeal, they were dismissed, while I was kept behind, like a naughty schoolgirl. Maestro Gracis was the first to attack. He told me that due to lack of rehearsal time and my inexperience, they had decided to recall the original soprano and ask the theatre to find me something more suited to my character. I was absolutely livid and unleashed my Irish temper, leaving them all in no doubt as to my ability to take on the part of Lady Macbeth, or any bloodthirsty role they might have on offer.

"I can understand you, Maestro," I said to the conductor. "You didn't want me in the first place. As for you," I lashed out at Puecher, "you assured me that all was well, when all the time you were hatching this plot behind my back."

I have never spent a more miserable Sunday as that one in Genoa. My stalwart friends in Milan told me not to leave the theatre without the situation being resolved. It might have been sooner if the theatre director hadn't absconded, leaving me to pay the hotel bill at my own expense. Technically speaking, I was still legally under contract to the theatre.

At last, on the Tuesday afternoon, I was summoned to the theatre, where the director was charm itself. They invariably are in these situations, but I knew him well, and was aware that, apart from being mortally humiliated, he was on my side. My supporters had warned me not to succumb to charm and, as the ball was in my court, I decided to hold out for the contract which suited me. It was the golden moment to choose something suitable for my "new voice". Having refused almost everything he offered, I finally chose three performances of Mahler's *Second Symphony*, to be conducted by the great Russian conductor, Yuri Ahronovitch, whom I had met socially at the home of mutual friends in Rome.

The director was astonished when I opted for the lower voice.

"But your voice is high."

"Ah," I announced, "now you are going to hear my new, low

voice."

The mortified man had no option; he knew I could have taken them to the cleaners and won. On the other hand, I knew that if I had taken them to court, I would never have worked again in the Italian theatre.

As I anticipated a lot of professional gossip about "La Wright's dismissal", I made sure that I got a letter from the theatre exonerating me from all blame. Such was the praise for my conduct that I could have used it as a suitable character reference anywhere.

When I returned to Genoa the following year, the circumstances and atmosphere were completely different. Ahronovitch, a Russian immigrant living in Israel, certainly lived up to his fantastic reputation as a flamboyant and dynamic conductor. He was more than surprised when, having given me the sign to enter for the soprano part, it emerged instead from my one and only colleague seated on the other side of the platform.

"You have a new voice; I like it," he exclaimed, after I let rip.

I just loved singing Mahler's music, especially with a conductor who knew how to get the best out of his artists and raise the audience to ecstatic heights.

There was an interesting sequel to this story: Years later, an American soprano friend of mine happened to be travelling on a train from Vienna to Venice with Ettore Gracis. Without realising that she knew me, he told her, completely out of the blue, how he regretted what happened to me in Genoa, since he had always respected me. It had obviously weighed heavily on his conscience over the years, while ironically, I was reaping the benefit of singing with my real voice as a result of being expelled from that particular production. The blame wasn't entirely his, since the artistic director should never have signed me up behind the conductor's back in the first place.

Suddenly, everything seemed to be happening. Although I never again had to scale such vocal heights as in *Hyperion*, my voice hadn't had a chance to stabilise itself. But I still managed to hold down jobs, unaware of the gossip going on around me. A visiting foreign singer told me that it was rumoured that my life was a mess, both vocally and mentally. With hindsight, I should never have taken this comment seriously, and now doubt its authenticity, because is truly out of character for Italians to gossip to a complete stranger behind one's back.

As I journeyed through life's rich tapestry, I discovered that people see mirrors of themselves in others. I later found out that this gentleman had his own problems and, like so many, was jealous of the wonderful rapport I had with Italians, whom I dearly love to this day.

Cancerians are very sensitive and vulnerable to this form of attack, so that I began to wonder if I really was a nervous wreck. There was no denying that I was under severe pressure, at home and abroad. By then my mother was in a residential home back in Ireland. I frequently visited it, often learning difficult scores while I kept her company. She was still fully in command of her faculties, and I confided in her about my personality crisis, and the strain of having to keep up out-of-character appearances.

"Do you turn up for rehearsals on time?" she asked. "Are they pleased with your work?" When I assured her that I did, my mother gave her opinion: "Well then, what you do and how you behave outside working hours is your own business."

How right she was.

One morning, Adriana Panni rang me in Milan from the Filarmonica in Rome to invite me to sing the role of the sorceress in a production of Purcell's *Dido and Aeneas*, with the great American soprano Jessye Norman as Dido.

Before I continue, I simply must tell you about Adriana. She was the most honest person one could have met in musical circles and, like myself, what you saw was what you got; a woman without frills or fancies.

She, with her daughter Luisa, ran the Filarmonica with supreme efficiency, and presented the Roman public with superb concerts by world-class artists. If it hadn't been for the Panni family, Adriana, her daughter Luisa and son, the conductor Marcello Panni, this book would never have been written, such were the openings and wonderful opportunities they gave me. Unfortunately, Adriana is no longer with us, but the Filarmonica is still carried on by Luisa.

It was because Adriana and Luisa had heard a deep colour in my voice, even before I would admit it, that they decided to show it off. One distinguished gentleman was so distressed when he heard I was going to sing the lower-voiced part of the Sorceress that he rang me up to enquire if Adriana and I had gone out of our minds. I told him not only to be prepared for a new role and voice, but a new hair colour as well: I had been accidentally transformed from a blond to the darkest colour imaginable, after a summer visit to a friend at her holiday home in Sicily when, in a slightly hungover state, we chose the wrong colour in a supermarket.

"Well," he continued, "as long as you haven't had a sex change, I wish you luck. I just don't want to see you ruining your career."

I confided to the English baritone singing the part of Aeneas that I had difficulty adapting my voice to the English text; he suggested that I should use a Belfast accent. It was instantly successful and released the voice, since Ulster vowel sounds are similar to the Italian ones, with which I had become so familiar.

On the first night, as I stood up to sing in my specially designed bat-winged dress, one could feel the tension in the audience, eager to hear the new Marjorie. On stage, we were simply honoured to be taking part in such a glittering occasion. This wonderful experience was summed up in the words of a colleague: "To think that we were paid to do this."

The next day I went straight to Florence to rehearse for a performance of *Commiato* three days later. It turned out to be another déjà vu scenario, similar to the one I had experienced in Venice and, ironically, with the same conductor.

At the first rehearsal my vocal chords were so physiologically blocked after singing such a low part in *Dido and Aeneas*, that I felt that I couldn't perform the work at all. The same thought struck the composer's widow, Laura Dallapiccola, after she read in the papers that I had been singing the part of the sorceress.

"How are you going to mentally and vocally adjust to such a contrasting change?" she anxiously enquired.

"I don't know," I confessed.

That weekend in Florence, instead of absorbing the beauty of that extraordinary city, I was closeted in my hotel room, once again afraid to face the conductor.

"It will be alright on the night," I assured this poor man, before whom I hadn't uttered one top note.

With hindsight, he had the patience of Job with me. If we had been pals, it might have been easier; but we continually seemed to be thrown together to perform impossibly difficult music under stressful conditions. It was then that I decided never again to subject myself to the misery of sitting alone in hotel rooms wondering how I was going to vocally survive. No career was worth it, and life was too short not to enjoy it. There and then, I made a decision: it was to be my last *Commiato*, and what better place to say goodbye than in Florence, where it was written, and in the presence of the composer's widow. Just before the concert, I rang her to tell her, and she agreed that I had done the right thing.

That evening, as I walked on to the platform, I was brought to my senses by the sight of the RAI TV cameras. Immediately, as in the first Austrian performance, the adrenaline began to flow, and I took off. It was judged to be my best performance of the work, possibly because I had been mentally freed from the fear of risking top notes.

Although delighted that we went out on a "high", I was heartbroken at singing farewell to my old friend *Commiato* which, having made my career, could have so easily ended it.

Chapter 7

The Crunch

Back home in Milan the landlord and his wife never did fulfil their promise of a contract. Instead, they put up my rent every quarter to maintain them in their spacious quarters round the corner, from where they kept a strict eye on my movements.

They, and my neighbours, were convinced that I was keeping a *casa degli appuntamenti* – the Italian translation for a brothel – because of the frequent visits of handsome young male students, who came and went from my house at hourly intervals. It so happened that my colleague, the American-Armenian soprano Cathy Berberian, had filled my studio with young talent, ranging from Italian pop stars, including the famous Giangilberto Monti, to the world of theatre. Giangilberto was so grateful for my help that he mentioned my name in an interview, following a big hit with Colombia Records, a gesture which makes vocal coaching so worthwhile.

I had a great time in the "flat from hell" with all these young people, who not only taught me about relaxing and letting my hair down, but saved me from the irreparable breakdown, to which, as tension mounted at an alarming rate, I turned a blind eye.

After yet another bizarre modern music concert, in which I performed the impossible works of an eccentric French composer – accompanied by the celebrated Solisti di Roma – I decided to take a break to reflect and settle my voice. It didn't last long, because a week later Peter Keuschnig rang. He desperately needed me at the Austrian radio in Vienna to sing two British pieces – unknown to me – by Harrison Birtwhistle and Anthony Payne. The latter was the English composer who so brilliantly wrote the conclusion to Elgar's unfinished last symphony, and husband of my colleague Jane Manning.

I particularly remember that concert because of my difficulty with the rhythms and pitch. Suddenly, Peter was inspired.

"Let's dance it," he suggested, meaning to move instead of performing, like percussion players, which, to the audience's delight, we did!

I was soon back in Vienna, to which I didn't dare travel without fish and special bread, made with oil. These were Milanese delicacies which my Austrian friends had sampled while visiting my home. On that particular visit, I sang the role of Isolde in a concert performance of *Le Vin Herbe*, by the Swiss composer Frank Martin, which we had performed the previous year with a merry group made up of soloists from Germany and the Vienna State Opera. They were such wonderful singers that they just lifted me to exalted heights; so much so, that the critics said that my voice was too strong for the Brahms Saal of the Musikverein. There were those who considered it to be adverse criticism, but when I tell you that the other lady, whose name was coupled with mine, became a renowned Wagnerian mezzo, I felt honoured to be associated with such company. One of the most frustrating aspects of performing classical music is that producers and conductors do not allow singers to sing from the heart with their real voices; it invariably has to be restrained and held within oneself.

Back on Italian soil, I decided to seek the vocal advice of Aldo Danieli in Venice. When I told him over the phone that I was wallowing in the lower part of the voice he nearly had a fit.

"You're mad. Come to La Fenice at once." The next morning, I took the train from Milan to Venice where I surprised even Aldo. He struck a note on the piano, and my response revealed my true voice.

"You're a mezzo!" he exclaimed. "If you've made a successful career with your voice turned upside down, imagine what you can do with it right side up". Aldo concluded that I had used the top of my real voice for so long that I had preserved my bottom notes.

Indeed, he predicted a good fifteen years of career left in me, which, to date, has continued longer than that.

One day, during a lesson in Venice, we had a good laugh when Aldo casually asked if I had found time to experiment with the singing tips he had given me.

"I think they are marvellous," I told him. "My students are certainly thriving on it."

"What!" he exclaimed. "You mean to tell me that you experiment on your students before trying it out on yourself; and, what's more, get paid for it?"

From then on, life jogged along in its usual bizarre way, until disaster struck. With hindsight, the bubble had to burst at some point. Pressure had been mounting for some time, and unfortunately took its toll on my nervous system, which I had imagined to be cast-iron. Salvatore Sciarrino decided to write an opera to show off both me, and my new voice, for the Biennale of Venice in September 1979. I was over the moon at such a prospect, since I had no engagements that summer and could devote the months to studying the new work. But, as the days and weeks flew by in the intense heat of Milan, not one page of the new opera appeared. In yet another déjà vu situation, I kept asking those who might have known his whereabouts where he was. "Writing the new opera," would be the reply.

One evening, to relieve the monotony of waiting, I decided to give my bathroom a good clean, adding a coat of wax polish over the marble floor to complete the operation. Before going to bed, I spread some newspapers over it so that my footprints wouldn't spoil my lovely gloss finish.

Next morning, woken from a deep sleep to answer the phone, I had a blackout in the bathroom, presumably caused by the strain of waiting for music, which never arrived. All I can remember is waking up in a heap on the floor to find, to my horror, that my foot was broken. In a state of shock, I crawled to the door and opened it, before screams for help were eventually answered by a neighbour. By the time the paramedics carried me down the stairs, my face, according to onlookers, was completely ashen. In the meantime, the entire apartment block had appeared on the scene, while outside, even bigger crowds had gathered to see the

'Irish *dame fatale* who favoured young men' being driven away. Such was the commotion that you would have thought I was going to the morgue. Never before have I felt so relieved to see ambulance doors being closed; but then they were immediately reopened, when the engine wouldn't start, to reveal even greater throngs. Eventually, a relief ambulance arrived to take me to a nearby hospital, where the break was confirmed.

My Italian friends were to prove that "a friend in need is a friend indeed". From then on, I was to experience kindness and hospitality, the like of which I have neither before, or since, experienced.

Stupidly, I had not insured myself against such unforeseen circumstances, and to relieve the strain of facing huge bills, the surgeon did a deal with me; I would give him English lessons in exchange for his medical expertise.

On waking up from the anaesthetic, I found that the hospital had already contacted a friend who helped me up onto my crutches, a gift from the hospital, before driving me home. I had an agonising time ascending the flight of stairs to my flat, to which my Italian friends soon flocked en masse with offers of assistance. To my shame, all I could think of was that I wouldn't have to learn the opera, although I could have fulfilled a concert engagement, seated on a chair, at La Fenice; but since feet are essential in Venice, I had to cancel it.

On that fateful day, I had the rare privilege of being fought over by friends gathered around my bed arguing about who should take care of me. In the end, it was decided that I should be shared. I was to stay with one family for a month until they were ready to move house. There I had a wonderful time being spoilt to death with specially prepared food, until the removers arrived to remove me as well as the furniture. The next two months were spent with other Italian friends who retained their daily maid for extra hours to wait on my needs. Lots of wonderful people visited me, among whom was a doctor friend of the family who was more than concerned when he looked at my plastered leg.

"I don't want to worry you," he said, "but if you look at your plaster it's crooked."

Sadly, he was proved right when it was removed after six long months. Another operation was considered but later abandoned, after it was decided that, as I could at least walk, it was better to let sleeping dogs lie. It also meant that my movements would be considerably restricted on stage, which really didn't matter, since future roles as a mezzo-soprano would be confined to mothers and nurses anyway.

In the meantime, I had to keep the wolf away from the door in the form of my greedy landlord, who by then was emotionally blackmailing me, knowing that alternative accommodation in Milan was impossible. And so, armed with my English teaching diploma, I was immediately employed on a part-time basis in various schools in the city, to which I sped along on my crutches, while people made way for me, or gave up their seats on public transport. Normally, I would have had to push and shove with the rest of them, in true Italian fashion.

It was also refreshing to meet people outside the world of music which, to my surprise, I didn't miss one bit. The Milanese work hard to make their city into one of the most affluent in Europe, and I taught all the hours God sent to accommodate these energetic people. Often they would have lessons before they went into their offices at 8 am, or on leaving them twelve hours later.

My friends couldn't help but notice how happy I was, but said nothing, as they knew I would return to the rat-race once I was relieved of my crutches. With hindsight, I was more financially secure because my lessons, along with my more substantial fees as a singing teacher, brought in regular money, whereas singing engagements, although well paid, had to last until the next assignment would show up.

It seemed that my enforced rest had been designed to show me a new way of living, and that singing wasn't, and never really was, everything to me. It meant, and still does mean, more to my friends who lived a more glamorous and enviable lifestyle which, if they had only realised, was over-hyped. What did thrill me was the great pleasure my adventures brought to my parents who, like so many Irish parents, had sacrificed much to give me a good education.

I returned to the world of music with a Bach cantata at the

Angelicum in Milan. The American conductor of that blissful piece was horrified to find posters round the city announcing my participation in a modern music concert.

"How on earth can you expect to sing Bach for me, while you're practicing that rubbish?" he demanded.

"I was just getting into training for you," I replied. But I loved the cantata so much that I introduced an American student of mine to it. She wasn't too pleased when she discovered that I was about to perform it in concert.

"You horror!" she cried. "Now I know why you were teaching me that work. You thought you'd kill two birds with one stone and save yourself study time." But I knew she would love it, forgive me, and include it in her repertoire, which she did.

One night this particular student rang me in desperation before her important concert that same night, to which the musical intelligentsia of Milan had been invited. One of the songs she had chosen was *Jeannie with the Light Brown Hair*, which exposed her broad American vowel sounds. There and then, we modified them, in what was to be one of my many telephone lessons, before setting out for the concert. As she got up to sing, a colleague seated next to me said, "Is that your student, Marjorie?"

"How did you guess?"

"Because you're halfway down your seat."

When a hair-raising incident took place, where else could it have been but Milan? Over a few "jars", I was persuaded to perform a new work by a young English composer, in which I was required to make wailing noises. Unfortunately, we didn't anticipate the conductor's mistake. He turned too many pages right at the beginning of the work, leaving us in complete disarray. Our natural instinct was to turn pages with him, but the ensemble's noble cellist stuck to his guns, ready to strike a chord which we would all recognise, once the conductor arrived at that point in the score. In the meantime, there was nothing I could do but keep wailing until we met up again. Even the audience was in stitches, since it was obvious what had happened.

At the end of the concert, when even the conductor thought it was funny, a distinguished musicologist, obviously unaware of the mess, congratulated me on the finest rendition of the work to date!

There is a postscript to this story. A decade later, when I happened to be telling a well-known agent about the incident, he said, "Is *that* what happened? The conductor told me that *you* didn't sing what was written."

Once again, another naughty boy had put the blame on me.

One of my greatest pleasures has been to sing with wonderful groups of instrumentalists from the principal orchestras in Northern Italy. There was the Gruppo Toscanni – recruited from the RAI orchestra in Turin – named after the famous conductor, of which my friend Gianpiero Taverna was in charge. Then the elegant Music Concentus, formed by the pianist Alessandro Specchi, and made up of players from the Teatro Communale in Florence.

We met through our mutual association with Luigi Dallapiccola, and had the honour of performing his works at his seventieth birthday celebrations in Florence. The maestro was rather taken aback that evening when a lady asked his wife if he was still composing. He retaliated by announcing that although a certain elderly composer was still composing the same old music, at least he was still composing!

When Dallapiccola died, Alessandro and I reflected on the blessed luck we had had to work with this great man who, in turn, had known and been influenced by composers such as Webern and Schoenberg, pioneers of the modern style of composition.

But the group with whom I had the greatest adventures was the Garbarino Ensemble, formed by the great Italian clarinetist Giuseppe Garbarino. Once again, it was through Dallapiccola's music that I met Giuseppe, when I was invited to sing with him and his group – made up from the Milan RAI orchestra – at the opening of the European University at Fiesole, just above Florence. It was a most amazing evening, in a glorious setting, providing such instant chemistry between us all, that Giuseppe invited me to accompany them on their forthcoming autumn tour of Scandinavia.

Initially, it fitted in with dates in Rome, where Adriana Panni had chosen me for the role of the nosy neighbour in two performances at the Filarmonica of Stravinsky's one-act opera *Mavra*. As you can see, Adriana good-humouredly knew how to cast me.

Everything went according to plan until I discovered that I had to do a lot of dancing, which made my weak ankle swell to ungainly proportions, causing much pain. To add to my problems, the mezzo-soprano – I was singing second soprano – had to be replaced at the last moment by a well-known Italian singer who, instead of getting on with the job, did nothing but remind us that she was practically sight-reading the piece. In yet another déjà vu situation, she swung round to me in the middle of a rehearsal and said, "You should have heard me sing Mistress Quickly at Glyndebourne." Having had enough, I turned round and retorted, "This is Stravinsky, not Verdi, where you have to count."

The final straw came when the two performances had to be postponed for two days to find a new conductor, after his predecessor's patience had been stretched to its limits by the histrionics of the female cast. He was replaced by an orchestral player, whose first words at rehearsal were, "Help me", which we did. The postponement sent the proposed Garbarino tour into chaos. It meant that instead of spending two days in Milan on my return from Rome to prepare my clothes for the tour, I had – if the opera finished on time – to catch the midnight train to Milan, repack my case, and make straight for the airport to meet the ensemble, bound for Copenhagen. To complicate matters, the train set off, not from the Central station in Rome, but one at the other end of town.

Back at Teatro Olimpico, my mezzo colleague had teamed up with our other colleague who, unknown to me, was beginning her campaign to have me thrown out of Italian musical circles. They made it impossible for me to share the same dressing room. I had to sit on the stairs outside the room until a special one was prepared for me.

Out on stage a battle of the posteriors waged, as the well-padded mezzo and I sat down on a bench, which she tried to push me off with her bottom. I was just recovering from one broken leg and certainly didn't want another, so I held on tight and pushed hard with my bottom until my territorial rights were reclaimed. I was just as bitchy as they were; but, it boiled down to the survival of the fittest, and I was learning fast.

After the final curtain call, I grabbed my belongings and headed straight for the train, stage make-up and all, where I jumped onto it, after the final whistle was blown. With perspiration rolling off me, I stupidly opened the window and caught a very nasty cold, as the train roared into the night.

Adriana had generously offered to fly me out to Copenhagen at her expense, if anything went wrong; but I arrived at Milan airport in time to join the Ensemble for one of the most thrilling experiences of my entire career.

I was very privileged to be the only non-Italian and, apart from the harpsichordist, the only female soloist in this merry group of superb musicians setting off on that Saturday morning for Copenhagen, *en route* for Oslo.

Our first lunchtime concert took place in the Sonya Henies Institute just outside the city. This modern building was built in memory of the famous ice-skater to display her numerous trophies and valuable paintings. It was, however, equipped with an air-conditioning system which made my condition worse. It seemed incomprehensible that this would be necessary in such a cold climate, until we were told that it was installed to preserve the treasures.

That evening, my throat was so sore that I wondered just how I was going endure a week of rehearsals and concerts, combined with plane journeys and changes of hotels. Fortunately, we were booked into a comfortable, old-fashioned hotel in Oslo, which considerably eased my suffering. Next morning, after a typical Norwegian breakfast of fruit and assorted cold meats, I braved the Baltic wind to look for a chemist, who gave me some effective pills which acted like dynamite on my throat and entire anatomy, with considerable success.

I spent a wonderful Sunday afternoon with Norwegian friends of my Austrian colleagues, sharing their main meal, which, in their home, usually takes place after the offices close around 4 pm. Darkness falls so early in these far northern countries that eating and working routines are different from ours.

Our next port of call was Stockholm, but not before I sneaked into the duty free shop at Oslo airport for a bottle of the "hard stuff" to act as a medicinal cure for my ailments.

Our accommodation in the Swedish capital was quite different from that provided in Oslo. There we were met by an official from the Italian Institute, who took us to their impressive headquarters in the diplomatic area of the city, where we were given a huge apartment all to ourselves. Stockholm is very expensive, and to eat out would have cost a fortune; instead, my Italian colleagues produced wonderful meals at the drop of a hat, while I did the washing up.

On our first evening we all went for a brisk walk along the waterfront, and I do believe that the sharp night air helped my cold. We were all enthralled with Norway and Sweden and the autumnal colours, to which, unlike me, the Italians were unaccustomed.

Our evening concert was held in the Italian Institute itself, where we were able to dress in our own rooms before walking downstairs to the concert hall. Later we were lavishly entertained to a wonderful meal on the premises, accompanied by night-caps. I gladly accepted a whiskey to relieve my cold. When I had swallowed the last drop, Giuseppe inquired if I would like another.

"Oh no," I said, "I have another bottle tucked under my bed."

My hot toddies saved my life, because I was more worried about letting down my colleagues than myself. Italy was a long and expensive way off to send for a replacement, apart from the fact that, being specialised, my programme was not in every singer's repertoire. The following afternoon, as we were taken to the airport, *en route* for Copenhagen, we couldn't take our eyes off the huge and extraordinary moon, already risen at two o'clock in the afternoon.

We arrived in Copenhagen in a downpour, and to a reception in sharp contrast to the previous ones. As our hotel was so near the air terminal, the taxi-drivers refused to take us there, leaving us standing in the pouring rain, surrounded by suitcases, percussion instruments, cellos – you name it. The chivalrous males of the ensemble carried the two ladies' luggage, while we walked through puddles to the hotel, which was hardly five star.

The following morning, I woke to find the previous evening's drenching had sent my cold right down to my chest. I was so anxious to conceal my worsening condition from the group that I avoided talking at breakfast.

"Marjorie is ill; can't you see?" they said to Giuseppe.

"Of course I know," he answered. "But she's a big girl. Just leave her alone."

Throughout the tour, his psychological approach to my precarious state of health had been a blessing. If he had unduly fussed or created a scene, as many would have done, I believe that my voice would have disappeared altogether from sheer fright.

My greatest challenge was that evening's concert. Fortunately, I hadn't used up all my Norwegian pills, while one of the gang brought me some equally effective inhalants, which we poured into a basin of boiling water, and over which, covered by a towel, we set to work. Once again, my Scandinavian medicine worked miracles, and by the time the concert came round, I was able to utter quite a respectable sound.

Our reviews were quite remarkable. One critic simply loved us all, while another slated me because I sang out of tune. We forgave him on the grounds that the sound of modern music must have been strange to his ears.

It was a pity that my coughs and splutters prevented me from exploring Copenhagen which, I believe, along with it's people, is really wonderful. As the Italians say, "It wasn't the moment".

After a short period of recuperation and regrouping, I was thrilled when I went with the Ensemble on a trip to England. It was a great opportunity to see some old friends and do some shopping.

In late October, we arrived at Heathrow on the early morning flight out of Milan, an hour ahead of English time. I felt very grand and superior in my role as unofficial guide and interpreter with, what I thought, was the perfect English accent. All went well until we reached Hyde Park Corner by tube – the heavy instruments were transported by cab – where I asked the way to the Italian Institute in Belgrave Square. "The Irish Embassy is down there," was the response. For the rest of the trip I was teased by the Italians about my "funny Irish English".

That afternoon we left for West Yorkshire to perform at the Huddersfield Festival of Contemporary Music which, under the direction of Richard Steinitz, has since grown into an international venue. The morning after the concert, we were waiting to board the train back to London when Giuseppe appeared with a pile of newspapers, all with reviews of our concert, one of which was full of question marks. Why hadn't they heard of us before? Why weren't there more people there to hear us? And where could a mezzo-soprano of my calibre be found. I nearly sent him my name and address!

All too soon the visit was over, but not before I had raided a supermarket for English goodies, unobtainable in Italy. At the top of the list were bacon and sausages, as well as some good tea, which I had missed.

While Giuseppe and the rest of the group went off to perform at another concert outside London, the harpsichord player and I held the fort at Heathrow, in case they didn't arrive on time for the flight to Milan. Alitalia was on time that evening. When the flight was called, we began to panic when our friends didn't show up, taking into consideration that percussion instruments and heavy equipment had to be loaded on board. I was just about to stage one of my histrionic scenes for the benefit of Alitalia, when a fleet of taxis drew up outside the terminal building, from which instruments were loaded at speed.

There was a disappointing ending when it was discovered that, with all the hassle surrounding our departure, I had left my sausages and bacon on a chair in the departure lounge. For an entire week afterwards, I didn't enjoy my breakfast thinking about what might have been.

A few days after our return to Milan, I set out with the Garbarino Ensemble to Innsbruck, in the Austrian Tyrol. Little did I know that it would be the beginning of a catastrophic turning point in my life, since it was during our recorded broadcast at the Austrian radio's studio that the first signs of nervous exhaustion appeared. Although my voice was perfectly in tact, my nervous system began to disintegrate. Not only did I lose my concentration, but I began making rhythmic errors, which had to be re-recorded.

From then onwards, pressures mounted; I found difficulty in coping with everything, from intricate music to even the simplest household chores; I was either on a "high", or in the doldrums.

Little did I know that it was the beginning of a serious nervous breakdown. Between singing engagements I sank into a deep depression, shut away from the outside world in my shabby flat. Strangely enough, throughout my ordeal, my voice showed no signs of my inner turmoil. I also had an answering machine, so that I didn't miss work, every lira of which went to meet the increase in rent demanded by my crooked landlord.

To add to my distress, my darling mother died on my birthday. I was so numbed that I obeyed her unselfish wishes and took my friends out for a meal to celebrate her life. It wasn't until a month after her death, when my accompanist, Rainer Keuschnig, and I went to lovely Lucca, a small town in Tuscany, to perform Mussorgsky's *Songs and Dances of Death*, that such poignant music unleashed my pent-up grief. Once again, Italian confusion nearly prevented the concert from taking place at all!

It was to be performed in a wonderful palace, in which Napoleon's sister had lived. Because it was open to the public during the day we were able to practice there unhindered. In contrast to Rovigo, we were welcomed by the organisers, so that we knew for certain that the concert would take place. Yet when we arrived there at 9 pm – half an hour before the start – the place was deserted. After a long search, we tracked down the relief porter, who denied any knowledge of such an event taking place. Only after we persuaded him to phone the authorities did he believe us. By that time, those who had turned up to hear us had gone off elsewhere; so Rainer and I, in evening attire, had to go out into the Square to retrieve them, and to awaken the interest of some stray tourists.

We had a great evening in such palatial surroundings, and were deeply touched when the Mayor of Lucca presented us with beautiful prints and books depicting the historic town. The following day, we went to nearby Pisa where, for the first time, I saw the Leaning Tower. So often a musician's life resembles that of an airline pilot, when work takes priority over visiting beautiful places.

After my mother's death, I had virtually lost my roots, leaving me with few remaining links with Ireland. Even the family home had been given up after my mother, assuming that I would never leave Italy, moved into a small flat.

During this time, visiting artists from England and other foreign parts were unhappy with the increasingly difficult musical situation in Italy. On their advice I began to expand my horizons, especially as I was beginning to feel the ground crumble under my feet. And so, armed with a repertoire suitable for a mezzo-soprano voice, off I went to Germany to audition in the main opera houses.

My first port of call was Munich, where the auditioning panel told me that I was a contralto, and not a mezzosoprano. Still in a state of shock, since it was my first audition with my new mezzo voice, I was advised to look for roles for an even lower voice, for which they had no vacancies.

The theatre in Gelsenkirchen, in the Ruhr valley, agreed with the Munich judgement, so that I was totally confused by the time I reached Frankfurt, on what was becoming a musical nightmare. While I was in vocal confusion, my friends, with whom I met up there, were even more shocked when the artistic director told me that my voice was too small for the Frankfurt opera house. It certainly was startling news, considering I was reputed to have one of the biggest voices in the business. Yet, the observant man who auditioned me did not dismiss me out of hand; in fact, he spent valuable time advising me on my future as a light contralto singing oratorio and lieder repertoire.

That afternoon we all gathered at a friend's house in the woods, outside Frankfurt, to recover from the shock.

"Let's see if he's right," suggested our host. Taking down a score of Bach's *St. Matthew Passion* he asked me to sing "Have Mercy Lord", written for the type of voice the discussion was all about. It takes a lot to subdue that merry lot, but after I had sung, there was a stunned silence. When we had all recovered the verdict was unanimous: "The man is right; Marge is a light contralto, and this is her music."

I knew it, too; in fact, I had always known it from my early days in Belfast, but throughout my career I had made the mistake of listening to others, instead of believing in myself. It took a long time to break this lifelong habit, but after my visit to Frankfurt I followed my own instincts, and took the first train back to Milan to reflect and regroup.

As my world tumbled around me, I struggled on. Still, it wasn't all doom and gloom. I was thrilled when the famous Italian avant-garde composer Franco Donatoni invited me to sing the first Italian performance of his work *Ultima Sera,* meaning "last evening". This work, one of the deepest and most poignant I have ever performed, drained me of all emotion. Usually, broadcasts from the Venice Biennale are pre-recorded and mistakes amended, but that evening I was unaware that it was live. Over dinner, I nonchalantly asked when the recording would be going out.

"It's already gone!" shouted everyone in unison.

Before he wrote this work, Franco asked me for my vocal advice regarding the heights and depths to which each type of voice could adapt; if other composers committed themselves to similar research, a musician's task would be considerably eased.

I shall never forget that evening in a Venetian palace, entirely devoted to Franco's music, when each artist had to give of his or her best to overcome the technical demands of this virtuoso piece, showing Franco's true genius. Sadly, he died in August 2000. Through my friendship with his family, he got to know me too.

One Easter Sunday, after a merry lunch sharing Irish jokes with his wife Susie, who came from Dublin, he saw the real, off-stage me, so different from the professional one he had known over the years. As we washed the dishes he said; "You must never lose the real you; the one who is so basically happy and carefree."

When I confessed that I had been in films as a funny girl, he and Susie immediately hit on the idea of my doing an Anna Russell-type of impersonation of well-known classical works. Many of the main theatres thought it would be a wonderful idea, but the musical establishment thought it might ruin my classical reputation. Sadly, the idea was scrapped because of snobbery; but when I later gained my musical freedom, I remembered his excellent ideas and incorporated them into my one-woman show *Music For Everyone,* which is still going strong today.

Before my health finally succumbed to pressure, I carried out two rather unusual singing engagements. Were any of them normal? I could count on my fingers the few that were.

The first was at the Vienna Festival, when I took part in the longest concert imaginable, appropriately called Marathon. It certainly lived up to its name, starting at 2 pm, after a heavy lunch, on top of which I had to sing, and which kept me going until the concert finished at ten. The event was in commemoration of the *Anschluss*, the forced exodus of the Jews from Vienna in 1938. It took place in a tobacco museum where the Jews had actually worked, overlooking the current state prison. It was ironic that the concert coincided with the presidential elections, and the announcement that the controversial Dr Waldheim had just been elected, causing Austria to veer to the political right.

I shall never forget my visit to the Festival of Montepulciano, the lovely hillside town in the divine wine-producing region of Tuscany, which is a popular venue for tourists. The story began one hot, sticky morning in August when I got a phone call from the English conductor Jan Latham Koenig, the newly appointed artistic director of the festival. From the sound of his voice, I immediately guessed that I was about to take off on one of my mercy missions – to rescue Mahler's *Second Symphony*, as it turned out. Apparently the Belgian mezzo had pulled out and someone had suggested my name as a possible replacement, without finding out if I even knew the work. The festival had another link for me, as it had been started by Hans Werner Henze, the composer of the opera in which the soprano went up in flames.

I asked Jan Latham Koenig when the performance was to take place.

"Sunday," he gently said.

"Sunday!" I yelled. "But it's already Thursday; my washing is dripping over the bath" – hardly the type of information a dignified singer should divulge to a conductor of classical music – "and I can't possibly leave until tomorrow."

That afternoon I sweated and ironed, as I struggled to remember Mahler's *Second Symphony*, which I had last sung four years previously in Genoa.

The journey to Chiusi, the nearest station to Montepulciano, practically involved a whole day's train ride; but the thought of leaving the city heat for the comparative coolness of the lovely hillside town filled me with delight. And so, on the Friday morning, I left Milan for what was to be not only one of the most amusing

142

weeks of my life, but one during which I suffered a ominous attack of homesickness.

The train was packed with people from the south of Italy, returning home from the industrial north to spend *Ferragosto*, the Italian holiday period, with their loved ones. From the moment of departure, they didn't stop talking about, or consuming, huge amounts of food, which they generously offered to share with me.

Just before we arrived in Florence, the engine broke down, leaving us to spend hours in open countryside in our airless carriages until a replacement arrived. Italians do not share my love of fresh air, so while I nearly suffocated, the windows were kept closed to avoid draughts.

The train was so late that I was concerned that those sent to fetch me would have gone home, as we were miles from any form of public transport. But when we eventually arrived, two charming young men from the festival were standing on the platform, ready to whisk me off to dinner, before escorting me to a family-owned apartment where I was to stay.

In mid-summer one expects to wake up to bright sunlight streaming in through one's window. Next morning I thought it was the middle of the night because the tiny window in my darkened room was high up in an alcove, making it impossible for me to read my music. In desperation I went to a bar in the main square where I had breakfast, before setting off for the rehearsal in a beautiful basilica, right in the heart of the countryside.

I needed to warm up before diving in at the deep end to rehearse with full orchestra and chorus, and a conductor whom I had yet to meet; so I ventured out into a field to entertain the awe-struck sheep and cattle. I'm sure that their ears were accustomed to such noises, as members of the orchestra were already blowing horns and trumpets in their pastures. It was all part of the relaxed and carefree atmosphere with which summer festivals are associated.

Back inside the basilica, I was panic-stricken at the thought of performing before a "home" crowd, made up from the Philarmonia chorus from London and members of other European orchestras, including the Royal Opera company of Covent Garden. But everyone was most supportive when they realised that I was standing in at short notice, including my colleague Teresa Cahill, who was accompanied by her partner, the composer Robert Saxton.

I realised what I was missing when the communal meals and camaraderie we shared together reminded me of my days back in London with the Ambrosian Singers. Everyone envied my washing facilities, because a breakdown in the plumbing system where the chorus and orchestra were staying meant that everyone had to wash in mineral water. When I tried to buy some to moisten my vocal chords, I was told that I was not an emergency case; toilets and cleaning purposes had priority.

I was overawed when Sir John Pritchard, the principal conductor of the BBC Symphony Orchestra, turned up to the Sunday morning rehearsal. When I told him that I was having difficulty remembering the Mahler symphony, he assured me that it would return by that evening.

That afternoon, between thunderstorms, lightning, a pianist who practiced scales non-stop in the room above mine until I knew his mistakes by heart, Mahler and I became reacquainted, after I appealed to the pianist. Poor chap, he was so apologetic, especially as he was going to the concert, that he offered me the use of his grand piano to practice on and vocalise. Italians are like that; it all comes from the heart.

Believe it or not, we, the artists, had difficulty gaining admission to the concert; but remember, this was Italy, where anything can happen. Teresa, Robert and I had just been collected from our abodes and driven to yet another glorious basilica at the bottom of an avenue lined with pine trees, and cars backed up, stretching as far as the eye could see. The conductor was immediately behind us in his car, otherwise, we might have been separated and the concert might not have taken place at all. There was even a police cordon preventing late-comers from entering the basilica.

I screamed and shouted in Italian that if they didn't let us in, there would be no concert. Fortunately for us, our local driver remembered a back entrance with an approach from an unused road, although a tractor would have been more appropriate. It wasn't so funny for Teresa and me, when we had to trudge our way over a muddy lawn in our evening shoes and dresses.

Inside the basilica throngs of people had gathered for the event, which was to be recorded for the RAI TV network. As usual, an announcement was made before the concert, in Italian, French, German and English, that I was appearing at short notice. I was surprisingly calm, until I heard the noise of the TV camera rolling beside me. But my worries were needless, because I heard later that the cameras had broken down during transmission, and we were never in the frame.

That evening, I decided to experiment with my new "cool" yoga-type approach to singing, and it worked like a treat. For the first time in my life, I hadn't used any emotional energy whatsoever, and there wasn't a dry eye in the house. To think that I had spent over twenty years of my life "socking it" to them, and it probably hadn't even registered.

The following morning we packed our belongings, ready to depart for Bolzano in the lovely Alto Adige. Teresa, Robert and I met in the village square where we were eventually spotted and conducted to a fleet of coaches parked at the bottom of a hill. Everyone was in fine holiday mood, relishing the wonderful scenery, as we sped on our way towards the Sud Tyrol. I was already familiar with the region, having spent two fantastic holidays at Ponte Gardena, just "up the road" from Bolzano, as well as performing at the same Bolzano festival, run by Dr Hubert Stuppner, who was waiting to welcome us there.

One has to be careful not to speak Italian in the Alto Adige, where one is encompassed by its incredible mountain range and the Dolomites reaching up to the sky. Because the region was once part of Austria, before being handed back to Italy after the Second World War, its inhabitants speak a German dialect. Although Italian is their first language at school, and they are Italian subjects, German is stubbornly maintained, while Italian, although understood, is rarely spoken. I felt rather unpopular when I would ask a question in Italian and receive a response in German.

Our elegant hotel was in the main square, within walking distance of the superb baroque cathedral in which Mahler's gigantic symphony was to be performed.

We were following in the tracks of the European Youth Orchestra, who had been there the previous evening with their conductor, Claudio Abbado; but to me, nothing could have surpassed our wonderful concert. The demand for tickets was so great that the concert was relayed to the crowds packed into the square to listen to Mahler's poignant music in the night-scented air.

Jan Latham Koenig's interpretation of this glorious work for massive orchestral forces, and a huge chorus bringing a thrilling performance to a mighty close, had an electrifying effect on those fortunate enough to be there. Thunderous applause ensued, to which we walked on and off the platform so many times that our feet ached, while our brows perspired in the baking heat. No performance of the work that I have since heard has ever measured up to that incredibly spine-chilling one in Bolzano.

The following morning we left for our final concert in Trieste, on the Italian-Yugoslavian border. It was a pity we didn't go home on the Bolzano crest of the wave, because the final concert turned out to be a monumental let-down.

The coaches, sent to collect us from Trieste were without air-conditioning and fitted out with the most uncomfortable seats I have ever had the misfortune to sit on.

No sooner had we left the outskirts of Bolzano than the driver announced that he had lost the way and, as I was the only Italian speaking person on the coach, it was left to me to interpret and mediate. Once on the right road, we all piled into a roadside restaurant for lunch, where the staff were so overwhelmed by the vast numbers of mouths to feed that many went without food. You can also imagine the long and chaotic queues for the limited number of toilets. Over our sandwiches, gallantly fought for by Robert, Teresa voiced my feelings.

"Do you think we'll have anywhere to sleep tonight?" she asked.

Towards late evening, tired, hot and hungry, we arrived at a hotel outside Trieste where, as we thought, we were all going to stay; but only the chorus had reservations, with no room at the inn for the soloists. Eventually, someone from the festival committee arrived, by which time the chorus was preparing for dinner. When they were asked if they would exchange their rooms to accommodate us, they graciously threatened to go on strike. So often one finds more prima donna-type histrionics in choruses and orchestras than with the real stars.

After what seemed an eternity, Teresa and I were loaded onto a coach taking the orchestra to another hotel in the centre of Trieste where, having queued up in another line outside the reception desk, we were informed that there was once again no room for Teresa and me. At that moment true British chivalry reigned supreme when two gentlemen from the orchestra gave up their rooms for us. Between showers and hair-washing we managed to grab a quick spaghetti in a nearby cafe, before setting off for the open air concert in the courtyard of the city's castle, overlooking the sea and the lights below.

The panoramic view may have been breathtaking, but there was no one to be seen. Neither was there a box office or anyone from the festival committee, except the man we met at the hotel, and even he had disappeared. There were seats laid out for the phantom audience, but nothing on stage to suggest that an orchestra and chorus were expected. Eventually, some members of the public filled up the vacant seats, and the concert got under way in unbelievable conditions. Many artists would have refused to perform, but we decided it wasn't worth the hassle.

While our singing was drowned by angry voices discussing the subject of money, smells from the restaurant wafted round Teresa. I was even less fortunate when petrol fumes, emerging from a contraption underneath my chair, found their way up my nostrils. In all, the whole event was a complete disaster from start to finish. Not being able to find any programmes, we assumed that none had been printed. I later found out, through the Venetian grapevine, that indeed some had been distributed, in which the name of Jan Latham Koenig had been replaced by that of a ballet dancer, who had taken part in a previous show in this invisible festival, held in James Joyce's adopted city.

Naturally, as news of financial squabbles reached our ears, we didn't expect to be paid. Teresa and I received our fee, however, when a generous soul dipped into his own pocket so that we wouldn't go away empty-handed.

Italy may be associated with corruption, but may I tell you that not once was my payment withheld. If, for any reason and for circumstances beyond one's control, a contract couldn't be honoured, it was immediately replaced with an even better one.

Undoubtedly, the summer months of 1982 were decisive. I knew the writing was on the wall when, as I was walking through the Galleria in Milan, an imposing-looking man stopped me.

"Marjorie Wright?" he said. "You have been in Italy for such a long time it's about time you joined our union."

It was as if I had just been approached by a thug issuing a warning: do as you're told, or else. It was clear that the worms, in the form of two nasty sopranos, which had so ominously crawled out of the woodwork during my first appearance at La Scala, hadn't gone away.

My worst fears were confirmed when I was approached about the possibility of singing in a new opera, to be performed the following May at the famous Maggio Musicale in Florence. Naturally, I gladly accepted such a prestigious invitation, and arrangements were finalised except for the music and contract, which never materialised.

One day, again in the Galleria, which is near La Scala and a meeting ground for those connected with musical life in Italy, I ran into a bass colleague who was also to take part in the opera. When I expressed delight at the possibility of working with him again, he had the embarrassing task of informing me that I had been replaced by an Italian singer.

I have always been regarded as a "nice" person who causes no trouble; but when I lose my temper, those who think I'm a soft target get an almighty shock. In the privacy of my own home, I lifted the phone and vented the full force of my anger on the person who, at that time, was in charge of this prestigious organisation.

"I hear you don't want me because the music is too difficult for me", I barked. "How can it be so when I haven't even seen it?" It was an ironic excuse, considering that I have made my name singing music which is beyond the reach of others. I ended my onslaught by telling the director what to do with his job, and that I would rather scrub floors than be involved with such people. I knew I had blown it, but I didn't care. Little did I know that it wouldn't be long until I would indeed be joining the world of Mrs Mops.

The crunch finally came when an agent from Vienna rang to ask me to deputise as the sorceress in one performance of *Dido and Aeneas*, conducted by the great Nicholas Harnoncourt, at the Salzburg Festival. I had previously auditioned for this major impresario during a visit to Vienna, when he told friends that although he liked my voice and presentation, he didn't know how to cast me, which was not unusual, because nobody ever has known. All my engagements have been achieved through word of mouth. It was only when I met this man socially that he saw the real me and realised that this was my part. Two days later, however, he rang me back with the news that the original singer had been able to rearrange her schedule, and that I was no longer needed.

I was bitterly disappointed, but, with hindsight, my health wouldn't have been able to take the strain of walking into a production and, with one rehearsal, going onto a world stage to risk my reputation, yet again.

By then, I had sunk into such a deep depression that I dreaded waking up the next morning to face yet another day, and all the stress that went with it. To ease my troubled mind, I spent hours devising a breathing method to eradicate stress. Let's call it "The Wright Way", which I have been able, through my teaching and writing, to pass on to those in trouble. My motto "Good comes out of bad" enabled me to emerge from that darkness.

Only my students kept me sane. That summer, however, and by sheer coincidence, they all found employment and moved on. Perhaps it was time for me to follow their example.

Hours were spent discussing the worsening situation with my Italian friends, who agreed that if I could work on home ground in England, without a bureaucratic rope round my neck, I should take the risk. In the meantime, they would keep the doors open for me; a promise which has been fulfilled to this very day.

I can sincerely say that I have never met more wonderful and genuine people as those I had the privilege to meet in Italy. Loyalty and friendship such as theirs are rare, and to be cherished.

My farewells were heartbreaking. All those lovely people,

immersed in love and passion from the depths of their Italian souls, could have provided the libretto for a wonderful opera, except that it was real.

On the day I left Milan, a distinguished Italian musician and his wife gave me the considerable fee which he had earned the previous night for one of his performances, so that I could start afresh. I vowed never to let them down. That commitment kept me alive when, back in the United Kingdom, friends turned their backs on me, and kicked me when I was down.

Chapter 8

The Road Back

To me, London was an escapist's paradise, and I basked in its anonymity. As if for the first time, I gazed in awe at this wonderful metropolis, remembering Dr Johnson's famous aphorism, "When a man is tired of London, he is tired of life; for there is in London all that life can afford."

My euphoric state soon evaporated when I realised that I had a made a huge mistake in returning to the UK, where the musical doors, so welcoming from afar, were firmly closed in my face. There was less work for singers than in the 1960s, when I had struck it lucky. Alas, if one hadn't influential contacts, then one could forget it. Without meaning to sound pious, I've never been a crawler and have achieved everything on merit. Even young singers were having a hard time, unless you won a competition to send you on your way. Realising that there was no turning back, I had to find a way to live in London and commute between engagements abroad. My problem was how to finance these plans. Usually, money up front is needed to fund professional engagements, expenses frequently having to be met before one is even paid.

My first task was to find employment and to remove myself from under the feet of my kind friends, who had given me a temporary roof over my head.

With Christmas approaching, I set off for Harrods store to join the queue of hopefuls filling in application forms with particulars of skills and previous employment. The officials were amazed when they saw my musical credentials and naturally wondered why I was there at all. I explained that I was "on sabbatical" to see how the other half lived, and they gave me a job over the holiday period in the hospitality department.

I assumed that I would be receiving interesting people and VIPs, but was soon brought down to earth when I found out that the hospitality section was where candles, artificial flowers and party goodies were sold to the rich and famous, while royalty, practically unnoticed, came and went. On one occasion, I was examining a credit card when I noticed an "HRH" on it and, on glancing up, saw a royal duchess waiting for it to be returned.

Harrods was just the medicine I needed. Not only was the discipline therapeutic but I learnt, after much patience on the part of the charming manager, how to work a cash till and write out credit cards.

There was a sense of camaraderie and humour among the staff, which was infectious. One morning, when I had a cold, I phoned in sick. Instead of being put through to my own department, the switchboard connected me to the funeral section. When I apologised for disturbing them, the undertaker said, "You sound much too healthy for us!"

"What a pity," I joked, "I could have got discount on my own funeral!"

Staff "perks" were an added bonus, and, with Christmas approaching, meant that I was able to indulge in delicacies from the food department, which I could not have afforded otherwise.

While gossip circulated in the musical world that, as a result of being thrown out of Italy, Wright had become a shop girl, I received a visit from a prestigious conductor who ridiculed me in front of other staff. I introduced him to the manager who graciously suggested that I should escort my colleague to the gentlemen's department. *En route* I told him, in no uncertain terms, that if he were to offer me a lucrative singing engagement, then I would give up my job in a store. Of course, it didn't happen, and our paths never crossed again.

I left Harrods after the January sales, and was deeply touched when they presented me with a box of delicious Belgian chocolates with a card wishing me luck in my new career. As what?

Before my departure from Italy, I had been invited to give a lovely lieder recital in Piacenza, a town outside Milan, in the valley of the River Po, where I had many friends and happy memories spent cooking, eating and drinking the delicious wine of that region.

Italians just love to invite family and friends to share their carefully prepared dishes with them. They are passionate about their food, and can spend hours discussing ingredients and how to cook them. Sunday lunches can last for the entire afternoon, after one has struggled through five courses; two would be enough for me. Yet it is a wonderful way to relax in the sun, and chat about nothing in particular.

My visit to Piacenza was morally uplifting. It was a wonderful feeling to return to a country where I was appreciated as an artist, from one where I was considered to be a has-been. The first thing that was universally noticed was the vast improvement in my health, which was attributed to a welcome break from the everyday hazards of the music trade. When I lived in Italy, my friends couldn't understand how someone like me, who outwardly seemed to be so gregarious and confident, could be so backward at coming forward, especially in the matter of asking for work and promoting myself. Over a period of time, they decided to give me lessons in self-confidence, which I gradually put into practice. When I was asked what people thought about me back in England, I said, "Arrogant and full of confidence."

"Well done," was the response. "Our lessons must have been effective; so keep it up!"

On leaving Italy, I was once again given a useful piece of advice. "Don't drop your professional dignity; clean floors and wait for the right moment, otherwise leave singing and rest on your laurels." Little did I know that, within weeks of my return to the UK, I would be doing just that.

Where and how I live has always been a problem throughout my nomadic career. Never having owned my own home, I have been dependent on landlords, and worse still, landladies. I was overjoyed when an ex-colleague visited me in Harrods – news travelled fast – and offered me temporary accommodation in her large house, just outside London. It wasn't long before I discovered that over the years she had become a rather embittered woman. She was so jealous of my students that she tried to intercept their phone calls, informing them that I had left the country. Fortunately, my so-called "friend" taught at a school during the day, while in the mornings, I was temporary housekeeper to her cranky bachelor doctor, who was looking for a suitable wife, a role to which she thought I might be fitted. But no such luck. For starters, his Victorian clothesline would have put any woman off the idea of matrimony. In spite of all these hazards, I had considerable freedom – when she didn't chain me out of the house at night – to practice my singing and look for alternative accommodation when the coast was clear. Things really came to a head when I was overheard negotiating a concert in Italy for my lieder duo with the organisers of the Monfalcone Wagner Festival. This innovative event takes place every year in this small town, in the region of Gorizia, near the former Yugoslavian border.

Before I left these Dickensian conditions for Italy, I still hadn't found anywhere to live, and, on my landlady's instructions, had to remove all my possessions from my room, which I was only too pleased to do, before setting off on my trip. I'm sure no other singer has had to deal with such problems while preparing for an engagement.

First of all, I had to transport my entire belongings, including household utensils, and deposit them in the left-luggage department of Liverpool Street station, before boarding a train for Harwich. There I caught the night ferry to Holland, *en route* to rehearse with my accompanist in Vienna. During the lovely train journey from Holland to Germany, passing through the panoramic Rhine valley on our way to Austria, I decided to forget my housing problems and concentrate on the job. With hindsight, I think it saved my sanity.

My Austrian friends were amazed at how, in spite of everything, I seemed to have jumped from one frying pan into another. They were even more incensed when I told them that some of my fellow musicians were rather delighted that I had "fallen off my perch". Indeed, if I had known what hostility I would face on my return to London, I'd have given up there and then.

Before this nightmare continues, let me cheer you up by telling you about the Wagner festival in Monfalcone and its wonderful organiser, Carlo Incontrera. Our collaboration was fun from the very moment Carlo rang me in London. Italians are great motivators and artistic adventurers, and Carlo was no exception.

While searching through the archives of Vienna University, he came across rarely performed songs of Alma Mahler, widow of the great Gustav. As Rainer, my pianist, was both Viennese and a graduate of this illustrious seat of learning, Carlo immediately thought of my lieder duo with Rainer Keuschnig.

We were also invited to perform the lovely *Rückert* and *Kindertotenlieder* of Gustav Mahler which, because I had sung neither before, involved considerable study. As enthusiasm mounted over the phone, so did the length of the programme. Many more pieces were added, including Wagner's *Wesendonck* Lieder, and works by Brahms and Hugo Wolf.

When Rainer timed our marathon with his stopwatch, he became increasingly alarmed, not only for my voice but for the length of the programme which the audience would have to endure. When I rang Carlo to suggest curtailing the programme, he said, "*Carissima*, last year we had Canino and Ballista, the well-known Italian piano duo, who played for four hours without encores."

"But Carlo," I protested, "they are pianists, while I am a singer!"

Even with cuts the programme was a singer's marathon, all of which I silently studied in my London bedroom. One could have cut the atmosphere in the house with a knife. It was unbelievable that people could be so jealous.

During that miserable period, I lost my faith in God. To this day, I cannot understand why he gave me a voice, and then made me suffer for it. Perhaps I'll find out at the day of judgement. One night, I was so unhappy and desperate that I turned to a photograph of my father, which I kept by the side of my bed. While I was praying to him, he winked to me with his left eye. I wasn't drunk, and didn't imagine it. Perhaps it was he who gave me the strength to go to Monfalcone.

During rehearsals in Vienna for the recital, I happened to meet an Austrian agent, when, naturally, the subject turned to the Italian concert. When I told him about the length of the programme he said, "How long does the Wagner festival last?"

"A week." I replied.

"Oh, thank God for that. I thought you were going to tell me that you were performing it all in one evening."

"We are," was my anguished reply.

We left Vienna for Italy on a glorious June afternoon, with the prospect of an exciting drive through northern Yugoslavia. When we arrived at the border I had the sinking feeling that I should have had a visa to pass through this country, as the customs officials ominously and thoroughly searched through my passport. It was a procedure to which I was becoming used once Belfast, my birthplace, was revealed.

On resuming our journey into Italy, we ran into an almighty thunderstorm, accompanied by enormous hailstones which battered against Rainer's ancient and beloved Audi. Then, on the Yugoslav motorway, an ominous sound coming from the engine made us realise that the Audi had not weathered the storm. Despite this, our old friend, which had carried us to and from many assignments, battled on at reduced speed until we drove into Monfalcone like a Formula One vehicle in distress.

Carlo and his friends, having just given us up for lost, were still at the restaurant where we had arranged to meet. When they heard the noise of the engine making its unforgettable entrance into the town, they ran out to welcome us. A firm friendship, already established by phone, was cemented over a wonderful spaghetti, washed down by delicious regional wine.

The Italian radio recorded our two-hour-long concert, which could have gone down in the *Guinness Book of Records* as the longest lieder recital ever.

Alas, the Audi had carried us on its last mission, because, on its return to Vienna, it went into semi-retirement, as a run-about for the wife of a friend of Rainer's.

When I got back to London, I temporarily booked into a bed and breakfast in Earls Court, accompanied by all my worldly goods. The money I earned in Italy would have easily covered the deposit on a flat, but I nearly lost it when my room was burgled. By a stroke of luck, I had converted the Italian fee for the concert into traveller's cheques, but some personal jewellery was also stolen, about which I was heartbroken. I suspected that the theft was an inside job, and took place while I was at breakfast. There was no sign of a break-in; if I hadn't gone to my hiding place on my return to my room, I wouldn't have known a thing about it. But, since I discovered the theft immediately after breakfast, I was able to run across the road to a bank and cancel the cheques.

With his staff under suspicion, Mr Patel the landlord was anxious to get rid of me and my accusations, so when a tour arrived he told me to leave at once, on the pretext that he needed my room. Without warning, at 10 pm, I was – metaphorically – thrown, bag and baggage, onto the streets. To be homeless, in the middle of London, without a soul to turn to, was the worst experience of my life, as if the ground had crumbled right under my feet. I was about to look for cardboard boxes when a complete stranger suggested that I should go round the corner to another Mr Patel, and see if he had any vacancies. This guardian angel helped me to transport my luggage to a hotel, which was, in fact, a Social Welfare hostel. As a paying guest I was lucky to have a room to myself, while entire families, assisted by the social services, had to eat, sleep and cook in the same amount of space.

To pay for a roof over my head, and to save my Italian money, I joined an upmarket cleaning agency, the same one which Princess Diana worked for before she met Prince Charles. It would take another book to tell you about my Mrs Mop career. I cleaned for the rich, the famous, the nasties, you name them.

One extraordinary lady, who worked for a bank, hired me the same day as the painters, so that I had to search under dust sheets to find the things she listed to be cleaned and polished. The burglar alarms in these exclusive houses really caused havoc and, because of my mistiming, brought the police to investigate on more than one occasion. This particular house was the like a tip. Once I had opened the front door, I had to run to the cellar to switch off the alarm, taking care not to let out the cat, which was as anxious to escape as I was.

The next was at the house of a former hanging judge in Knightsbridge, where I was hired to look after his wife, who was recovering from a stroke. She was perfectly behaved until I took her in her wheelchair to Harrods, where she regulary went raving mad, screaming and shouting for attention. Having worked there myself, my heart went out to the staff having to endure such abuse. I was relieved of my services when I injured my already vulnerable ankle, after a piece of masonry fell on it on my way to her home. It was as if a warning had been sent down from heaven.

In the intense heat of that summer in 1983, I encountered all types of womanhood, from the spoilt, the intolerant to the impossible. One rich American lady, living in Belgravian splendour, wouldn't let me touch her bed until she had measured the exact position of the sheets. I was eventually dismissed from her employment when, having been stuck in a traffic jam, I turned up at her house ten minutes late.

My worst experience was when I had to wash clothes by hand, because the washing machine had broken down. They belonged to an American pop idol, of whom, closeted in my classical world, I had never heard. He and his vocal coach were on film location in London, and had rented a flat in Sloane Square. Of course, they didn't believe me when I told them that I was also a singer and vocal coach. True to form, it wasn't long before I was sacked from that job too, after I vehemently denied breaking a mirror. But I didn't go quietly. My parting from Sloane Square was worthy of a West End stage production, when I was ordered to carry the rubbish down to the basement.

"Carry it yourself," I yelled at the egomaniac, as I made my exit to the accompaniment of some unrepeatable language. While I was waiting for the lift, outside the front door, I overheard the two men talking.

"What a woman"! one of them said. "Maybe she is an opera singer after all. She sure acts like one."

I was sorry to be dismissed from one Chelsea lady's service, because she had been very nice to me. It must have been difficult for her to tell me that her husband, who was a chinless wonder, simply couldn't stand my exuberance at the breakfast table, and I would have to go. Before I left she surprised me by saying, "It will be alright, you know; I've been there as well. It will take another two years to recover, and when that happens, give yourself a big pat on the back."

How true her words turned out to be.

The turning point in this chaotic way of living, in which I was experiencing how the other half lived, came when a commercial traveller overheard me asking the hotel manager how long I could stay. The rep, who was actually selling beds to the hotel, told me that his boss had a flat in the east end of London which would be ideal for me. There and then, he took me to an area of the city which my friends would, and did, scorn; but it was a bargain at the price and, after all I'd been through, seemed like heaven. The contract was signed on the spot, and the following day I moved into my first London home, from where life evolved in a way that I could never have imagined.

London's East End gave me space in which to think and breathe, and a base upon which to build a firm foundation. Eastenders are blessed with a cheerful disposition and a no-non-sense attitude to life, reminding me of Ulster people; they pro-vided me with a sanctuary, conveniently accessible to London, in which I spent many solitary soul-searching hours.

I shared the Victorian terraced house with a young couple, who lived in the downstairs flat with their son and their cat, Agamemnon, in whom I confided. As we shared a common entrance hall, I was often invited in for a cup of tea, over which we discussed our very different lifestyles. Until they got to know me, I was considered to be rather toffee-nosed and a Thatcherite, in contrast to my young friends' world of Hell's Angels and other bikers.

After I joined the ranks of the unemployed, we helped each other out until the next giro arrived. In the meantime, I struggled to get back into the world of teaching singing and English and performing, for which I was qualified.

One morning, while holding forth in the "Soch office", a lady accused me of holding up the queue. When I tried to answer her as politely as I could, she turned round to her cronies and shouted: "So this is what this country has come to, when we have a grand dame teaching us how to speak posh like Maggie Thatcher!"

I still suffered from frightening panic attacks and nightmares about being homeless, which even haunt me to this day, although they gradually subsided as I began to fill my life with things to do.

Concentration was my greatest difficulty, after my mind had lost all sense of co-ordination. To correct this, I began knitting Aran sweaters, which required intricate cabling and counting. Because it wasn't music, I was able to establish a certain theme of continuity. I wouldn't wish mental illness and depression on my worst enemy. One feels ostracised from society, for the simple reason that others cannot cope with the embarrassing symptoms. For the victims it is a lonely road; only they can find a solution to end the trauma.

All through this rehabilitation period I couldn't bear to listen to a note of music, switching off the radio at the very mention of the word "concert". It was a long time before I could even enter a musical venue, let alone sit through an entire opera, or any form of musical entertainment. My doctor's diagnosis was "burnt out". Yet, with his help, I battled through this traumatic period without a tranquilliser or any other form of medication; instead, my recovery was due to sheer willpower and positive thinking. I learnt to avoid the "downers", who told me that I was a woman on my own, I was too old, and would never make it back. With hindsight, I had, up until then, done more with my life than those who were condemning me for hitting hard times, an experience which makes one a stronger person, once survival has been achieved.

As an unemployed person there were many schemes one could take advantage of. The course for which I opted was a dressmaking one, which I just loved. We had a fabulous teacher who was on good terms with the dress fabric shop opposite our venue. There I found the most wonderful materials at wholesale prices which, combined with Vogue patterns, made up into some stunning outfits.

One day, our landlord came to see us with the devastating news that he had received a substantial bid for the sale of the house, with vacant possession. We were offered an enticing sum of compensation money, which we all accepted. I had already been considering a flat in Putney, in the process of refurbishment, which would provide me with the "right" address, and proximity to the people whom my friends thought I should be cultivating to further my career.

Deep down, I was sorry to leave the East End, the place where

I wrote the first draft of my book; where I had a brush with the law after I reported a suspect happening to the police, only to be arrested myself and released from a cell, inside which I sang excruciating top notes for three hours, until an officer on the next shift took pity on me. The whole matter was conveniently brushed under the carpet, but when I was later called upon to serve on a jury, I took the part of the defendant against the police, who had unlawfully entered his home without a warrant. The man was bad news and was going down anyway on another offence; but having experienced what it was like to be unfairly judged rather influenced my judgement.

And so, after more than three adventurous years in the East End, I once again packed my bags and headed for temporary bed-sit land, until my flat was ready. If I had known what was in store, I'd have stayed put in East 17.

Despite never-ending domestic turmoil, the tide had turned, and for the better. I got a job teaching English to foreigners in an Oxford Street school which, although exhausting, was exhilarating and brought me into contact with so many nationalities, all with their special speech problems. The Japanese had trouble with their "Ls" and "Rs", while the Italians had difficulty in pronouncing "th". One delightful Japanese girl told me that "John McEnroe was praying at Wimbledon." We corrected it by saying, that "He was praying that he could play at Wimbledon". On my birthday she sent me a lovely card wishing me a "memorial" birthday. Laughing and teasing was an effective and enjoyable way of learning English quickly.

Gradually, the spoken word became my great passion, with days spent reading, writing and researching new material. This I found in abundance when I applied and was accepted for the post of vocal coach at a school for actors near Richmond. There, I taught young people to sing who hadn't a note of music in them, yet were willing to absorb everything I knew.

During my first term, in a tiny theatre by the river Thames, I, in collaboration with Larry Dann – the celebrated TV actor who once played the Sergeant in the police drama *The Bill* – was required to prepare these kids, in a limited space of time, for a specially written Ken Hill musical.

After hours of laborious rehearsals, I would simply crawl home, but we managed to put on a successful week of shows, during which my clinic was set up to soothe weary voices and shattered nerves. So inspired was I by this feedback, and Larry's expert directing, that I at once set to work on my singing manual *How To Be A Bad Singer*, which I later followed up with another book incorporating tips and advice for actors, stammerers, preachers and others who required vocal coaching. Writing saved my sanity, while concert performing took a back seat.

I was very sad when I was made redundant from the school. Unlike my Mrs Mop enterprise, I wasn't sacked; it was purely a financial measure.

To ease my frustration at not being able to get my teeth into anything connected with the world of music and drama, along with distinguished colleagues, I hired a room at the Wigmore Studios. My new group of friends introduced me to rock and pop artists who were concerned about preserving their vocal chords. While most of my fellow teachers were producing mellifluous sounds from their flock, mine were belting it out. My own voice improved from training talented showbiz artists from another side of the vocal spectrum, those normally scorned by more classically trained singers. I also realised how restricted I had become from conforming to the more conservative approach to classical music.

It was through my new connections that I socially met stars like Angie Bowie and Buster Blood Vessel, the lead singer of the then top of the charts band, Bad Manners, who inspired me with new vocal ideas. Without doubt, this was one of the most productive periods of my life, and I was simply enjoying every moment of it. I was being rejuvenated and introduced to a world of forbidden musical fruit, which I had only read about in magazines.

Although my bouts of depression were diminishing, as a result of occupational therapy, I still had my bad days. A breakdown is not something which heals overnight; and, with hindsight, I count myself lucky to have recovered so quickly. Some sufferers never do.

Meanwhile, a friend decided to take matters into his own hands, and made an appointment with a faith healer. So desperate was I to relieve my state of mind that I agreed to see her. It wasn't until I got there that I realised she was also a clairvoyant.

While I sat in the sitting room waiting for my turn, a great feeling of peace came over me. What was to follow was unbelievably accurate: that I had been guided into a society and career, to which, although artistically suited, I was unable to adapt. I was just a normal, everyday person trying to fit into the wrong niche.

I already knew that I was surrounded by jealous women who envied my lifestyle as a singer. Little did they know of the trials and tribulations into which my voice, which had become a burden, had led me. My late mother used to say that a singer needed a skin like a crocodile and the hide of a rhinoceros.

In this extraordinary session, the psychic saw a typewriter, books and a new life, once troubled waters had been calmed. On my next visit to her I asked, "Do you think it is worthwhile continuing my career?"

"It hasn't even started yet," was the comforting reply.

Although I was aware there was a long way to go, light was beginning to appear at the end of the tunnel.

In 1985, through a brief association with a management, I was engaged as a classic artiste on the *QE2* to commemorate the fiftieth anniversary of the maiden voyage of the *Queen Mary*. Such an opportunity filled me with excitement. Not only was I mad about ships and the sea, but I had never been to America and the Big Apple.

I had only a month to prepare a completely new programme of the music of the 1930s, including Gershwin and Cole Porter, liberating my voice from the more elitist world of Schoenberg and Britten. At last, I could let rip in mid-Atlantic, with everyone in holiday mood.

When I arrived at Southampton docks with Judith Ginsburg, my young Canadian pianist, the Queen Mother was lunching on board the *QE2*. Naturally, we had to wait until the band of the Royal Marines played her off the ship to Gershwin's *Foggy, Foggy Dew*, already setting the scene for the songs we had chosen.

By the time Judy and I boarded the ship, the weather had turned into a grey, dismal late-spring afternoon, indicating unfavourable conditions. One almost needed a map to find one's way round the huge liner, but Judy, with her keener sense of direction, was the perfect guide.

As we were tucking into our first meal, a waiter, with a dead-pan expression, announced that we were about to run into a storm. We thought he was joking, but he wasn't. The following morning, we woke up to an ominous roll in the ship's movement, and by midday both Judy and I were feeling decidedly unwell.

We were scheduled to perform only twice on the five-day voyage to New York; the first on that very Sunday evening, with the second the following Wednesday afternoon. To prevent sea-sickness, I went down to the ship's clinic, where a number of off-colour passengers were queuing up with the same idea in mind. When I told the nurse that I was performing that same evening, she insisted that both Judy and I should be given injections. What she didn't tell us was that, while they might ease our nausea, they would completely knock us out. If I hadn't set the alarm before we slept the day away, we might have been still in the land of nod, instead of performing.

Before going down to the theatre, we got into our 1930s period clothes, which I had borrowed from a friend who owned an antique shop. We had hoped to warm up before the performance, but the theatre was also used as a church and cinema. Being Sunday evening, a service was in progress when we arrived, so we had to wait our turn until the faithful departed.

In the meantime, the storm had reached hurricane proportions, and the ship, built to avoid such a battering, rolled from side to side, not only exacerbating our already groggy state, but providing horrific performing conditions. I consoled myself with the fact that even the mighty *QE2* was suffering in obedience to Mother Nature.

Just as we were going up the steps at the side of the stage, the ship gave one almighty dip to one side, throwing me backwards, down the stairs, and onto my posterior. My screams brought the entertainments director to the disaster area. He anxiously enquired if I needed anything.

"A brandy," I implored.

The combination of the drink and injection was both instant and dramatic: as the boat swayed from side to side, so did I, prompting me to announce to the equally groggy audience –

164

many of whom were reliving the same trip, made fifty years earlier
– that I wasn't drunk, but feeling rather under the weather.

With this sense of nothingness, what was supposed to be a classical act developed into a cabaret. As my voice and memory cells
parted company, I had to make up my own words. I was so desperate, that I invited the audience, who were more familiar with the
repertoire, to join me in an impromptu sing-song, which they just
loved. Judy couldn't believe her eyes or ears at this Marjorie whom
she had never seen before; it was as if I had taken off on a flight
of fancy. Certainly it wasn't the concert we had intended present-
ing. At the end, I felt so embarrassed that I implored Judy to lead
me back to our cabin, and out of sight. *En route*, we passed by the
lounge where the famous American harmonica player Larry
Adler, also swaying from side to side, was explaining to his admir-
ers that he was feeling rather sea-sick.

As we groped and swayed our way round the liner, we were
stopped by a group of Americans who enjoyed our show so much
that they insisted on buying us a drink. They all came to our next
concert, which took place in calmer waters and without further
mishaps. We were determined to redeem our artistic reputations,
which was rather ridiculous, considering that we were in the
middle of the Atlantic, where nobody could have cared less.

As the liner sped on its way to New York, the weather improved,
enabling us to enjoy walks on the promenade. I wallowed in the
luxury of the leisure centre and swimming in the smooth, velvety
water of the pool before breakfast and dinner; it helped reduce
weight gained as a result of indulging in the wonderful food
which Cunard provided. We were soon brought down to earth
when a weather report was pushed under our cabin door, informing us that we had run into growling icebergs off Newfoundland.
As memories of what happened to the *Titanic* invaded our
thoughts, Judy read out yet another communique, announcing
that we were also 400 miles off course.

"What are we going to do?" said Judy.

"Well," I said, in my no-nonsense Ulster logic, "if we are going
down, at least it will be on the *QE2*, with all flags flying."

During our many trips up and down the ship's lifts, we ran into
some of the TV crew who had been contracted to film a documen-

tary of this memorable crossing. Apparently, they had accidentally dropped in on our hurricane-inspired show because they were too early for the film following our gig. They told us that they regretted not being able to include us in their documentary, as it would have been hilarious. Perhaps it was just as well, as deep down, although I love a good laugh, I am interested in serious and soul-searching material.

We were scheduled to dock in New York on the Thursday morning, but due to the unexpected weather conditions *en route,* we were a day late, enjoying extra time on board as the guests of Cunard.

Judy and I were not due to fly back to London until the following Sunday, so we had time on our hands; but other passengers were not so happy. The ship was scheduled to go on to the Caribbean after we had disembarked in New York; so it was decided that, instead, we would dock at Baltimore to pick up passengers waiting to embark there for the Caribbean. Those who had been on the maiden voyage of the *Queen Mary* were furious at the prospect of missing out on the joy of reliving that enthralling experience of sailing up Upper New York Bay, while passing the Statue of Liberty and the fabulous Manhattan skyline simply because rich passengers might have to miss a stop on their trip to the West Indies, due to our late arrival in the States. We, on the other hand, were just thankful for a safe deliverance from the cruel sea.

As we were disembarking at Baltimore, we saw a fleet of hearses waiting by the quayside; apparently, some of the elderly people on board, reliving the maiden voyage of the *Queen Mary*, had sadly not survived the tempestuous storms.

Five years later I was invited back by Cunard to reverse the previous trip by boarding the *QE2* at New York, and sailing to Southampton. On that occasion I was treated as a VIP, in my role as a writer and lecturing on my book, *How To Be A Bad Singer.* But my singing act was still remembered by some crew members who invited me to remain on board at Southampton for one extra night, to entertain those who were waiting to sail on to more exotic places.

Both trips were experiences of a lifetime, which I shall never forget, and hope to repeat.

On my return to London, Rainer Keuschnig and I gave my first and only recital in that great metropolis, at the Austrian Institute, in Knightsbridge's exclusive Rutland Gate. I was more than apprehensive at performing before so many distinguished people from London's classical music circle; but I forgot about them, once I began to sing the wonderful songs of Gustav Mahler and his wife Alma, I was transported into another world.

At the reception after the concert, everyone was most complimentary, both of my voice and interpretation, but deep down, I knew that nothing would come of it, however well I had performed. Before I left London for Italy, I had failed eight auditions at the BBC, and, obviously, the situation hadn't changed. I realised, from the frosty atmosphere, that my personality simply didn't fit into the more conservative-type category which they, and other British musical establishments, preferred. It reminded me of the old days in the Ambrosian Singers, when the cry was, "What a pity Marge can't quite make it here; what a waste of talent; what a loss to British and Irish music."

Before I left Italy, I naively imagined that my track record abroad, which was well known among British musicians, may have gained me some recognition in England and Ireland; instead, I ended up on the dole, where I remained for many years. I was forced to admit that, from the professional point of view, I had made a terrible mistake returning to the UK.

My collaboration with some of the world's most powerful musical establishments simply counted for nothing back on home ground. It was obvious that my Irish personality was an embarrassment to more conservatively groomed people who, alas, were in control of my career.

I had a similar experience when I eventually moved into the long-awaited flat in Putney, owned by the widow of a famous radio personality. When it was discovered that I was not a Tory, and Irish as well, attitudes soon changed; so much so that, once again, I had to pack my bags and leave. In Italy everyone revelled in my Irishness, but back in the UK I had to defend my own folk like an ambassador.

One kind friend suggested that I should contact the Royal

College of Music with a view to giving back to others some of the knowledge with which I'd been endowed while abroad; but the eyes of those in charge just boggled at my ideas. I left the building where I had spent three years studying a method I had since discarded, feeling a total misfit.

Everyone was most charming, and could certainly not be blamed for being rather overcome by my enthusiasm and pioneering ideas. Even the BBC, who, when they recorded the world premiere of *Commiato*, had assured me that all those nasty auditions were in the past, had changed their mind. When I contacted the them on my return to London, I was informed that as such a long time had elapsed since that memorable recording, I would have to audition yet again. And so, *Commiato* was to be both my debut and swan song for that great seat of broadcasting. Slowly but surely I was discovering that you can't win them all.

After further unsuccessful attempts at infiltrating the ranks of the English National Opera and the Royal Opera, I gave up the struggle, although I did enter into written agreement with the Royal Opera when we exchanged invoices for twelve copies of my first book.

"They wouldn't employ me as a singer, but they have me as a writer," I said merrily. Who knows? Perhaps they were right.

After so many fruitless efforts, I decided to put singing on ice and concentrate on my great love; writing. It was obvious that my off-stage gregariousness was too overpowering to fit into the confines and intellectual aura surrounding the world of classical music. Eventually, I found my own down-to-earth musical setting, about which you shall read as my tale approaches the last act.

You will also be relieved to hear that, from then on, life took an uplifting turn towards less harrowing and more productive times. It seemed that, at last, I was on the road back to happiness and normality.

Writing, through which one can be transported into another sublime, exciting world, can also demand hours of solitary confinement. I'd had my fair share of this during my singing career, so when a friend suggested that I should apply for the advertised job of cloakroom attendant at Raffles nightclub in Chelsea's Kings Road, I jumped at the idea to financially support my exciting venture into the unknown. The manager was Italian and just loved singers; how could I have not been accepted?

Raffles's premises must have once been an elegant period house, with an old staircase and opulent oak doors, the theme of which had been cleverly incorporated into the club's decor, leaving the customers with the impression that they were spending an evening in a typical country house-party setting.

Raffles was fun from night one, and when I wasn't relieving someone of their coat, or seeing that the loos were clean, I just loved looking out over the busy night life of the Kings Road from my chair by the side of the front window. I took up residence in my secluded quarters around 10 pm and, while waiting for my customers to arrive, I would either write, or proof-read what I had written. Many of the ladies who passed by my table were famous writers and gave me the most useful tips and advice, before depositing a tip into my little dish, with the word "thank you" delicately stamped onto an equally delicate piece of porcelain.

Night after night I gradually became an agony aunt, advising young ladies on the type of young man who might be worthy of them, while wiping the tears of those who had just not found "Mr Right". This was rich coming from me, with my track record of broken romances. My advice ranged from, "He's a jerk", to "Bleed him dry". But it was all great fun, especially being driven home by taxi to Putney at 3.30 am, or having early breakfast with a friend in a Chelsea cafe.

When friends in Norfolk suggested that I should rent a flat in their Norwich property, I embraced the idea with enthusiasm. Things were neither working out on the domestic nor the professional front in London, and it was time to move on, yet again.

The atmosphere of cathedral cities has always appealed to me, and lovely Norwich was no exception. My first summer there was idyllic. Inspired by the famous Broads, the expanse of flat countryside and the unbelievable skies and sunsets, I plotted my next move. Norfolk haunted me, especially in winter when dark skies seem to hang over one. Then suddenly the clouds would disperse to reveal an amazingly clear sky. It was as if I too had been caught up in its spell, which even determined my moods.

Springtime is especially beautiful in that part of the world, when the cherry blossom and magnolia trees are in bloom. Being a nature lover I just absorbed everything this atmospheric countryside had to offer. Whenever I needed a spiritual uplift, I went along to the cathedral to listen to its magnificent choir and organist. At night, this wonderful building is breathtakingly impressive, when floodlit and viewed from afar. Unfortunately, this haven of beauty did not yield up spare-time employment to keep the wolf from the door, so I was forced, while putting the finishing touches to *How To Be A Bad Singer*, to once again join the dole queue. However, it turned out to be a blessing in disguise.

At that time there was an amazing programme called the Enterprise Allowance Scheme, enabling one to start one's own business, for which a £1000 loan was needed. Having still kept my account with the wonderful Allied Irish Bank in London, I persuaded them to back me, which they did. And so, equipped with my loan, I joined the ranks of those willing to take a risk in life, and began my own business as a self-publisher.

How to publish the book was the greatest problem. My friend Jenny courageously typed it, my rock student drew cartoons to relieve the monotony of reading about anatomy and singing technique, while other friends, who owned a stationer's shop, printed it. Three weeks later, on Guy Fawkes Day, it was launched in Norwich, heralding the birth of a new era in my life.

Given its home-made production, the thought of selling it to a bookseller had never entered my head, since I had only considered using the book for lectures and workshops. Then one day, when I was down in London with a friend, we happened to pass by Hatchards, the Royal booksellers in Piccadilly.

"Why don't you go in and ask them if they would like your book?" she suggested.

"What?" I exclaimed. "You must be joking."

I had hardly uttered these words, than my friend pushed me inside, where I tentatively approached the buyer, who was most interested in my book. The following week I returned to Hatchards where I made out an invoice for twelve copies.

My humble offering left much to be desired in the way of finesse, compared to the beautifully bound volumes in front of me; they made me realise how presumptuous I had been to even approach the buyer of such a prestigious establishment, let alone "flog" my home-made book to him. That invoice from Hatchards meant more to me than any singing contract I had ever signed. It was both a new challenge and an indication that there was life after singing.

Every singer has to face the fact that one day their career will come to an end. Sadly, there are those that admit that performing hadn't been worth all the disappointments and nervous tension, so necessary to achieve excellence. If it hadn't been for such traumatic moments in my singing exploits, I would never have become a writer.

With Christmas approaching, there was a great demand for one-offs like mine, so that by the time I sat down to the festive cheer, I was already an established author, with my books on sale in Foyles, Hatchards, Boosey and Hawkes, the Royal Opera and Waterstones, where it sold particularly well in their South Bank store. Of course there were those buyers who questioned the home-made presentation and poor material of the book, while others considered the title to be too over the top. When I explained that it was chosen while I was describing the contents to a serious solicitor, on how not to get into bad vocal habits, they changed their minds.

The only problem was that the sales flow was held up while I waited to be paid by the retailers; money without which I could neither repay the bank loan nor buy new materials.

One day, while I was on my sales round, one of the buyers advised me to find a publisher who could market the book for me. As I lived in Norwich, he suggested that I should get in touch with Bill Elkin, whose firm was based there. This I did, and a few weeks later a contract was signed with William Elkin Music Services, while I retained my position as sales rep, which I loved.

My friend Riccardos made the accompanying cassette to the book at his Anagram studios in Norwich, transforming it into a complete DIY kit, in which I sound like a book at bedtime reader, with hardly a trace of my native accent.

In 1989 *How to be a Bad Singer* was officially launched, back home in Ulster, at the Newry Arts Festival, where we had a wonderful evening, attended by old friends whom I hadn't seen for years.

Owing to the low profile I maintained during my breakdown, many had been concerned about my whereabouts and had tried to find me over the years. There was a round sigh of relief that I was still in the land of the living, especially in Warrenpoint, which I hadn't visited for nine years. During that time, great changes had been made, transforming the affluent town into a thriving port.

Some time earlier I had discussed the possibility of eventually returning to Ireland, preferably within reach of the sea and, more importantly, an international airport. The time had come to live in a place I loved, and where I felt at home, as opposed to locations which offered work opportunities.

During that "Warrenpoint Revisited" visit, as I looked out over its incredible scenery, an overwhelming sense of nostalgia and homesickness swept over me. There and then, I decided to return some day to this lovely spot; little did I know that it would be sooner, rather than later.

In the meantime, I journeyed round Ireland promoting myself on radio and television chat shows, including *Kelly*, on Ulster Television, Pat Kenny's morning chat show on RTE; and Sean Rafferty's morning chat show on Radio Ulster.

On the morning of my departure from Dublin airport, a local taxi-driver – Dublin's taxi-drivers are both sharp and literate – recognised me, and said: "Aren't you the bad singer?" He was referring to the book, not my singing, since I hadn't sung a note during my visit to Dublin. There is nothing worse than performing to one's home crowd. Generally, I am more composed when confronted with perfect strangers, because I know, once airborne, I shall probably never see them again.

Spurred on by new and exciting challenges, I devised a new show which could be adapted for lectures or entertainment purposes. The idea came to me after my over-the-top concert on the *QE2*, when I discovered that I could reach out to real people, from every walk of life, who, as long as it was well presented, would enjoy whatever I sang.

Not long after my book launch, I went up to Yorkshire to sing at the wedding of my friends' son. It was my first visit to this heavenly part of the world and, as the train journeyed past York on its way to Malton, near Scarbourough, where my friends own the most glorious home, I felt that my late mother was very much with me, enjoying the scenery which she had loved so much. Before her marriage she had taught, walked in the dales, and played golf in that homely county.

Margaret and West de Wend Fenton then lived in a Palladian mansion in miniature now owned by their son Jonathan, in the North Riding of Yorkshire. Ebberston Hall has been described by Hugh Montgomery-Massingbird as England's smallest stately home. Their son and his bride Jane were married in this idyllic setting overlooking the Vale of Pickering, in true James Herriott country.

The village church at Ebberston is literally at the bottom of Margaret and West's garden and driveway, where deer and pea-cocks wander about, in keeping with this rural, away-from-it-all atmosphere. Henry, their giant turkey, named Paxo by Jane when naughty, took rather a shine to me. He even took time off from guarding the house to chase me round the grounds, much to everyone's amusement.

The launching of my new career happened to coincide with media attention on Ebberston Hall, for which funds were needed for restoration. As I too was in need of restoration, Margaret and I decided to put on my new show in the same church, proceeds from which would go towards the appeal fund for the Hall, while I had the ideal setting to launch *Music For Everyone*.

When the pianist "chickened out", West suggested that I should play for myself; so we hired a keyboard, on which I made my debut as the accompanist I had always wanted to be. It gave me a great sense of freedom, as I was able to dictate my own speeds and rhythm in my own good time.

I shall never forget that wonderful evening. The church was filled to capacity, and afterwards everyone went back to the Hall for a candlelit supper. It was also the night when the Irish football team reached the quarter-finals of the World Cup in Rome, news of which was relayed to me during the course of the evening. We lost, but nevertheless, like all other Irish people who didn't want to miss a good party, we toasted their success at having done so well.

In 1991, immediately after my return to Norfolk from the second trip on the *QE2*, I put on a similar venture in the village church at Castleacre, not far from Norwich. Norfolk is famous for its large number of amazingly beautiful churches, but that one, in the most attractive location, alone and surrounded by well-kept lawns, is a joy to behold.

When I told my friends there about my new show, they had a chat with the vicar, who initially had grave doubts that anyone would come. After much discussion, he and I made a deal; the proceeds would be divided between me and the church and, if nobody turned up, we would entertain ourselves, as no expenses were incurred anyway. And so, with nothing to lose, we started our PR campaign.

We thought that the best time to have the concert would be during the flower festival, another Norfolk speciality. As excitement mounted, the vicar discovered that he had considerable talent in the publicity department; so much so, that extra seats had to be brought in to accommodate the crowds, who piled into that lovely church on the most perfect May evening imaginable.

Although feeling slightly jaded after my trip to New York – and all the parties I had attended – I was on top of the world that evening. Inspired by the homely audience, I told some funny stories surrounding the songs, which ranged from Mahler to Cole Porter. Not only did they go down a treat, but news spread round East Anglia that my concerts were a must, "because of the craic", as they would say at home in Ulster.

At last, I was beginning to sing how and what I liked, although some of my former colleagues did not agree with my opinion, that if one doesn't put passion and feeling into the music of Bach and the great classics, one can vocally and technically end up in strangulated knots. But then, I'm biased, since I just love Bach, and sacred music in general, considering them to be the most direct route to Heaven.

The following year, in 1992, my friends informed me that they had decided to take over the entire house in Norwich to accommodate their family. This meant that once again, I had to pack my bags.

It so happened that on my many trips down to London by

coach, I became friendly with the most delightful and fun-loving lady named Diana, who is blessed with "the sight". Even today, when we speak on the phone, I enquire, "Is that real or a 'tinkle'?"

One evening as I waited for her at Victoria coach station to board the coach back to Norwich, she suddenly appeared in a rather animated state.

"Marjorie, you must go back to Ireland," she said. It's all waiting for you there. You're wasting precious time here."

I had to admit that she was right. I had been considering returning there anyway, so what was the point of postponing it indefinitely? As fate would have it, when I went over to Ireland to set the ball rolling, at the beginning of 1992, a beautiful flat came vacant in Warrenpoint. Ulster people don't hang around, which meant that an immediate decision had to be made. At that time, I was inclined to dither, but after so many urged me to "go for it, and come home", I did exactly that.

By sheer coincidence, I discovered that I had chosen a home overlooking the back of the house in which Percy French, the composer of the famous song *The Mountains of Mourne* had allegedly lived.

It meant that this story had gone full circle; from the day that I made my childhood singing debut beside the Percy French statue in Newcastle, to my present-day existence, where the Mountains of Mourne really do sweep down to the sea.

Encore

Northern Ireland was just what the doctor ordered. My problems paled into insignificance compared with the horrors suffered by many of the people of Ulster. At least my family was still intact, while others who had lost theirs, even found it in their hearts to forgive. They are an example to us all.

Despite the Troubles, there was an air of progress and economic buzz around the province, in comparison to the deep recession in the rest of the UK at that time. I was immediately helped by well-wishers, relatives and friends, who arrived at my lovely new home laden with household gifts.

After years of being dominated by overbearing landlords and landladies, it was sheer bliss to have my own front door and letter-box. Having my business exposed to neighbours and property owners had become rather tedious, to say the least, especially when my giro arrived to "lower the tone of the establishment".

My home in Warrenpoint was a maisonette, with only two garages underneath, so that I had no neighbours either above or below; I felt like someone who had just been released from behind bars, being able to come and go without my every movement being watched.

In 1979, while still living in Italy, I gave a concert of contemporary music with my kinsman, the pianist Michael McGuffin, at the renowned Belfast Festival at Queens. I had established such a warm rapport with this superbly run organisation that, on my return to Ulster, I dropped into the festival house to say hello to

Michael Barnes, the then director, and his assistant Robert Agnew. While catching up on the news, I happened to mention to Michael that I was enjoying choosing repertoire for my new show *Music For Everyone*, never imagining for one moment that he would include it in his festival programme. Throughout my career, people have always had difficulty in casting me at auditions. "We like the voice," they would say, "but we've no idea how to cast you." Only when we meet informally am I given work in which I can express my true self. And so it was with Michael, who just jumped at the idea of a mixed bag of music, ranging from Mahler to Van Morrison.

Blessed with this wonderful stroke of luck, the Irish premiere of my one-woman show took place in November 1991 in the Harty Room of the beautiful Queen's University of Belfast, near where I was born. The hall was packed with familiar faces, some of whom I hadn't seen since my naughty schooldays. After the concert, they greeted me with, "You haven't changed a bit!" meaning that I was just as mad as ever. I was very nervous making my debut as a pianist in Belfast; but after the glowing introduction from Robert Agnew – who later succeeded Michael Barnes as artistic director of the festival – a relaxing and a happy evening followed.

Spurred on by such a warm audience, I lapsed into my storytelling mood, which extended the programme three quarters of an hour over time and caused havoc with parking meters. I got the best write-up of my career; it stated that now I was back home, more should be heard of me. Unfortunately, the novelty wore off, and once again I was subjected to lamentations, with "the prophet is not without honour, save in his own country" – her, in my case – being added to "what a pity".

Three years later I "dusted" my voice and, with Robert as the festival's director, my new one-woman show *Requiem for a Diva* was premiered at Belfast's Lyric Theatre, as part of the mini-fest of the Festival at Queen's.

I only had to go "up the road" to Newry to find the ideal producer for the show in Sean Hollywood, director of the award-winning Newpoint Players, who was so sadly and prematurely taken from us during the writing of this book. Sean and I went back a long time, and only someone who had known me could have directed the show with such expertise. At the last rehearsal, when I asked him if everything was okay, he said: "The only thing that would worry me is that you might 'take off', and we'll all be there for breakfast."

My old pals at BBC Northern Ireland also rallied round. No sooner had I landed home on home soil that Sean Rafferty, whom I first met when he interviewed me in Rome, invited me to take part in his morning chat show, where one just met everyone who was anyone. Then Gerry Anderson, who was filming his summer series *Anderson on the Road*, interviewed me both on his radio and TV chat show at beautiful Rostrevor, two miles away from my home.

I met Gerry again a few months later, when the BBC thought it would be hilarious if I could teach him to sing *The Ugly Duckling* on their *Children in Need* programme. It was certainly entertaining, but then Gerry is a true professional, which made him the ideal student. To publicise my latest one-woman show, I was given a spot on the highly rated *Patrick Kielty Show*. Because it was at prime viewing time, when the whole of Ireland seemed to be glued to their sets, I felt I had reached the height of my career when I was recognised in supermarkets!

Being able to join in and share community joys and sorrows was most therapeutic. For a short time, I played the organ in the local church, opening doors to wedding invitations. Irish weddings are a great excuse for a "day out", and a night as well, as often they don't finish until well into the following day.

My birthday party, that first year at home, lasted for four days. It was a wonderful feeling to be accepted for what one is. Although, like any small community, people are interested in the "goin's on" of others, one is allowed one's privacy, which to me, after the back-biting of the music profession, was sheer bliss.

I felt I had really arrived home when I appeared at the Warrenpoint International Festival under the heading, "Local Artiste". I was thrilled to be accepted back into my home town, and kept the poster up on my wall to remind me of the importance of one's roots.

I was very honoured, on my return to Ulster, when I was invited to distribute the prizes at my old school in Newry. Because I wouldn't have won the prize for former model pupil, I spent the afternoon telling the students about what a naughty mischief-maker I had been.

But the crowning point in my home-coming was when I was invited to present the prizes at my old school. When I sang and accompanied myself in a Rossini aria and a Schumann lieder I realised how far we had all come, from the day the Boss created a special musical opening for me, to the thriving present-day musical department at the school.

In retrospect, I was fortunate to work at a time when there was an abundance of concerts and recording sessions, and to have shared privileged moments with famous people, who gave me so much to hand on to others.

Opportunities, for which others would have yearned, were handed to me on a plate; in fact, I was thoroughly spoilt. One sensible colleague said, "You know, Marge, I am getting tired of musicians saying that you have 'missed the boat' and are unlucky. You decided to take up singing, and won a scholarship to the best music college imaginable. Then you went to teach at one of the best schools in England. Tiring of that, you joined the best group of singers in the world, before abandoning them to go to Italy where you ended up in the best opera house and concert platforms in the world. When you decided to perform and lecture on a ship you ended up on the *QE2*. So don't tell me that you are deprived and unlucky, because it isn't true."

After so many trials and tribulations, my lot is now a happy one. On a return visit to Italy some years later, I was overwhelmed to be tracked down by Teatro Massimo, in Palermo, where I had performed my first opera. They had heard I was in Rome and thought I would be perfect for the part of Mistress Quickly in Verdi's *Falstaff*, to be performed there two weeks later. Obviously someone had dropped out at the last minute. I was flattered that they had remembered me after an absence of twenty years from Palermo. Unfortunately, I had never sung the role, which, given time to study, would have been ideal for me; also, the thought of having to learn it at such short notice brought back the old sense of fear which had caused my illness. It was at that point that Ornella, my agent in Rome, brilliantly brought the operatic side of my life to a fitting conclusion, when she advised me to say no to the heavy, stressful side of singing by going out on a high, having just refused an offer from Teatro Massimo, where I had performed my first opera. Furthermore, the operatic stage had never been my scene, so it was pointless to prolong the agony.

It wasn't the end, but a regrouping of singing for me, as well as administering vocal therapy to those with vocal and breathing problems.

You may like to know what is happening on the Italian front. The doors were left open as promised. In 1999, I went on a "fire brigade" mission to Genoa to coach some fine Italian singers in a production of Benjamin Britten's *Rape Of Lucretia*. While I was there I made enquiries about the "two ugly sisters", one more powerful than the other, who so successfully aborted my career. Although retired from their singing careers, they are still making life difficult for those – including Italians – who cross their paths. If a student leaves them, they will destroy them. How, I don't know; but I hope to find out some day, when I shall be able to put the last pieces of the jigsaw together. When I do, I shall feel like Cinderella reclaiming my glass slipper, even if the clock has long since struck midnight.

So watch this space, and I'll let you know.